The Des Moines Register COOKBOOK

A Bur Oak Original

The Des Moines Register
COOKBOOK

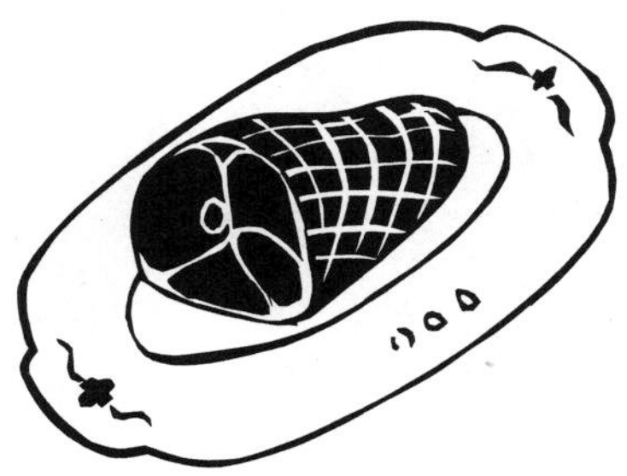

By Carol McGarvey,

Marie McCartan,

and C. R. Mitchell

University of Iowa Press  Iowa City

University of Iowa Press, Iowa City 52242
Copyright © 1995 by Carol McGarvey, Marie McCartan, C. R. Mitchell, and the Des Moines Register and Tribune Company
All rights reserved
Printed in the United States of America

Cover illustration by Beth Krommes
Design and text illustrations by Karen Copp

No part of this book may be reproduced or utilized in any form or by any means, electronic or mechanical, including photocopying and recording, without permission in writing from the publisher. The recipes in this book have not been tested by the publisher.

Printed on acid-free paper

Library of Congress
Cataloging-in-Publication Data

McGarvey, Carol
The Des Moines Register cookbook / by Carol McGarvey, Marie McCartan, and C. R. Mitchell.
p. cm.—(A Bur Oak original)
Includes index.
ISBN 0-87745-515-5 (pbk.)
1. Cookery. I. McCartan, Marie. II. Mitchell, C. R. III. Des Moines Register. IV. Title. V. Series.
TX714.M383 1995
641.5—dc20 95-13459
CIP

01 00 99 98 97 96 95 P 5 4 3 2 1

Contents

Preface

For years, cooks across the Midwest have clipped recipes from *The Des Moines Register.* Tattered and stained from use, these recipes have been copied and shared and sometimes lost. But here they are again, all together and updated for the nineties. It doesn't matter if you're a budding gourmet or just an everyday cook, you'll find recipes here to make gatherings with family and friends memorable.

We've included some vignettes written by Carol McGarvey, who relates some of her interesting experiences as a longtime food writer and columnist for the *Register.*

Take some time to browse through the book—the recipes range from the simple to the sublime, from Artichoke Rumakis to Luscious Lemon Treat. Many of the dishes have won top prizes at the Iowa State Fair. Our Party Planner chapter offers something a little extra—festive menus plus step-by-step timing to follow as you prepare for a big event.

Our recipe testers and our best and toughest critics are the thousands of devoted readers of *The Des Moines Register* Food Pages.

Happy cooking!

Acknowledgments

The authors gratefully acknowledge the good Iowa cooks—and the far-flung friends of Iowa cooks—who have shared their favorite recipes over the years.

For delicious personal contributions in the way of recipes, we want to thank free-lance food writers and cooking experts Mimi Gormezano of Iowa City and Linda Hodges of Ames.

Also offering good food and good help were a number of *Register* colleagues: Eliot Nusbaum, art critic and resident gourmet; Tom Kollings, columnist, outdoorsman, and campfire cook; and especially Jennifer Phelps, a copy editor who volunteered her time and skills as well as her recipes.

Other colleagues who helped with their special talents included artists Tom Weinman and Todd Hanson; Russell Karns, newsroom production technology assistant; John Gilmore-Baldwin, programmer-analyst; and news assistant Kyle Munson.

Also, for their expertise and inspiration, we thank the following: Iowa State University Extension Service (Patricia Redlinger, Elisabeth Schafer, Margaret Van Ginkel, and Susan Klein), ISU AnswerLine, Iowa State Fair (Kathie Swift and Arlette Hollister), Iowa Beef Industry Council, National Pork Producers Council, Iowa Pork Producers Association, Iowa Egg Council, National Turkey Federation, Tone's Spices, Meredith, Ruth Mitchell of Hy-Vee, Family Features, California Tree Fruit Agreement, Dole, Rice Council, Kraft, Pillsbury, General Mills, Duncan Hines, Betty Crocker, Bisquick, Softasilk Cake Flour, Crisco, Campbell's Soup, T. Marzetti, Reames Noodles, Jell-O, Sure-Jell, Electronic Color Editorial Services, Fleischmann's Yeast, Gold Medal Flour, National Dairy Board, Midland United Dairy Association, Quaker Oats, Nestle's, Hershey's, Rhodes, and Pace, among many others.

Last but by no means least, we thank Jean Tallman, former food editor of *The Des Moines Tribune*; the late Dorothy Yeglin, *Register* food editor; and the late Pat Cooney, who wrote market basket features for the *Tribune*. They led the way in proving it was OK to be journalists and mothers at the same time.

The Des Moines Register
COOKBOOK

Starters

Chili con Queso

Tasty patio treat

1 (1¼-ounce) package onion soup mix
⅔ cup milk
2 cups shredded Monterey Jack, Muenster, or Cheddar cheese
½ cup tomatoes, chopped
1 (4-ounce) can chopped green chilies, drained
½ teaspoon chili powder

In 1-quart casserole, thoroughly blend soup mix with milk. Microwave on high 1 minute. Stir in remaining ingredients. Microwave on high 2 minutes or more, or until cheese melts, stirring after 1 minute. Serve warm with tortilla chips, bread wedges, cooked chicken chunks, broccoli, or cauliflower. Makes about 2 cups.

Lemon–Poppy Seed Dip

A light dip for strawberries

⅔ cup nonfat sour cream
5 teaspoons honey
1 tablespoon lemon juice
1 tablespoon poppy seeds
1½ teaspoons finely grated lemon peel

Blend ingredients. Serve with fresh strawberries. Makes 6 servings.

Low-Fat Spinach Dip

Just right for grazing

2 cups low-fat cottage cheese
1 (10-ounce) package frozen chopped spinach, thawed and drained
1 (1-ounce) envelope dip/salad seasoning mix
2 tablespoons reduced-fat sour cream

1 clove garlic, minced
⅛ teaspoon hot pepper sauce

Combine ingredients in food processor or blender; process until smooth. Chill. Serve with vegetable or cracker dippers. Makes 2¾ cups.

Speedy Chili Dip

Easy party fare

½ pound lean ground beef
½ cup chopped onion
1 or 2 garlic cloves, minced
1 (6-ounce) can tomato paste
½ teaspoon chili powder
½ teaspoon flour
¼ teaspoon ground cumin
¼ teaspoon salt
¼ cup shredded Cheddar cheese

Crumble beef into 1½-quart microwave-safe casserole. Add onion and garlic. Cover loosely with waxed paper and microwave on high 3 to

5 minutes or until beef is no longer pink, stirring once. Drain fat. Stir in remaining ingredients except cheese. Cover loosely with waxed paper and microwave on high 3 to 4 minutes or until just heated through. Sprinkle cheese over top and microwave on high about 1 minute longer, to melt cheese. Serve with corn chips or tortillas.

Vegetable Wreath and Dip

See Champagne Brunch for Twenty-four, p. 233.

Blue Ribbon Salsa

From Pat Hatch of West Des Moines, Iowa

3 cups fresh tomatoes, chopped and drained, or 1 (28-ounce) can tomato wedges
½ cup thinly sliced green onions
2 jalapeño peppers or 1 (4-ounce) can chopped green chilies, drained
¼ cup chopped celery
½ teaspoon salt
½ teaspoon leaf oregano
⅛ teaspoon pepper
2 tablespoons vegetable oil
1 teaspoon grated lemon peel (optional)

Combine ingredients. Store in refrigerator or heat to boiling and pour into hot sterilized pint jars and seal. Process 15 minutes in boiling water bath. Good with raw vegetables, crackers, and chips. Makes 3 pints.

Green Tomato Salsa

Good way to use green tomatoes

3 medium-sized green tomatoes, coarsely chopped
½ cup onion, finely chopped
2 jalapeño peppers, seeded and minced

1 medium clove garlic, finely chopped
¼ cup fresh cilantro leaves, coarsely chopped
¼ cup fresh parsley, coarsely chopped
½ red bell pepper, coarsely chopped
3 tablespoons lime juice
1½ teaspoons sugar
Salt to taste

Place tomatoes, onion, jalapeños, garlic, cilantro, and parsley in food processor or blender. Blend to coarse puree. Add bell pepper, lime juice, sugar, and salt. Blend well. Serve with vegetable dippers or chips. Makes 1½ cups.

Apricot-Brie Torte

12 ounces cream cheese, softened
¼ cup apricot brandy or apricot nectar
⅔ cup toasted walnuts
½ cup dried apricots, finely chopped
1-pound wheel Brie cheese
Apricot nectar, for brushing on torte

In food processor fitted with metal blade, process cream cheese and apricot brandy or nectar until smooth. Add cooled toasted walnuts and process until nuts are chopped. Add dried apricots and pulse until apricots are combined with cream cheese mixture. Cut cold round of Brie in half horizontally. Place bottom half on serving plate. Spread half of apricot–cream cheese mixture on top. Place second half of Brie on top, with "skin" side touching apricot–cream cheese mixture below. Spread remaining apricot–cream cheese mixture on top. Cover with plastic wrap and refrigerate.

Torte may be served as either appetizer or dessert. As appetizer, top torte with toasted walnut halves. As dessert, top it with small wedges of fresh apricots, arranged in concentric circles. Either way, brush with apricot brandy or nectar just before serving to give torte finished, shiny appearance. Serve chilled. Makes 12 to 16 servings.

NOTE: To toast walnuts, place in single layer on baking sheet; roast at 350 degrees until nuts are toasted, about 5 to 10 minutes. Watch them carefully, because they burn easily.

Breakfast Strawberry Spread

1 (8-ounce) package cream cheese or light Neufchâtel cheese, softened
2 teaspoons sugar
½ cup coarsely chopped strawberries

Mix cream cheese with sugar until blended. Stir in strawberries. Spread on toasted bagels. Makes 1⅓ cups.

Layered Strawberry Spread

1 (8-ounce) package cream cheese or light Neufchâtel cheese, softened
1 cup sliced strawberries
¼ cup orange marmalade or strawberry preserves, heated

Place cream cheese on serving plate. Top with sliced strawberries. Drizzle heated marmalade or preserves over top. Use as spread on toasted bagels. Makes 8 to 10 servings.

Peach Melba Bagels

Bagels
Cream cheese or light Neufchâtel cheese, softened
Red raspberry preserves
Fresh peach slices

Spread cream cheese on toasted bagel halves. Top with preserves and peach slices.

Pâté on Apple Slices

See Champagne Brunch for Twenty-four, p. 232.

Smoked Salmon Pâté

From Mimi Gormezano of Iowa City, Iowa

5 ounces smoked salmon
½ cup melted unsalted butter
2 ounces cream cheese, at room temperature
2 teaspoons Dijon-style mustard
3 tablespoons sour cream
1 tablespoon vodka
2 to 3 teaspoons fresh lemon juice
3 tablespoons minced fresh dill
Freshly ground pepper, to taste

Place ingredients in blender or food processor and blend until smooth. Add more mustard and dill to taste. Cover and refrigerate several hours. Mixture can be used to fill cherry tomatoes, small pastries, and deviled egg halves or as a spread. Makes 1½ cups.

Salmon Mousse

1 (¼-ounce) envelope unflavored gelatin
¼ cup white wine
½ cup boiling water
¼ to ½ cup reduced-fat mayonnaise
1 tablespoon lemon juice, freshly squeezed
1 tablespoon onion, grated
½ teaspoon Tabasco sauce
½ teaspoon paprika
1 teaspoon salt
1½ pounds cooked salmon or 3 (7¾-ounce) cans salmon, flaked

1 cup whipping cream, divided
2 tablespoons fresh dill

In medium bowl, sprinkle gelatin over wine. Let stand 5 minutes. Add boiling water and stir until gelatin is dissolved. When cool, add mayonnaise, lemon juice, onion, Tabasco, paprika, and salt. Stir to mix well. Set bowl in large bowl of ice cubes until mixture reaches consistency of egg whites, about 10 minutes. Lightly grease 4-cup mold. Remove any skin and bones from salmon. Place salmon and ½ cup of cream in blender or food processor and puree. Mix in dill. Fold salmon puree and dill into slightly thickened gelatin mixture. With wire whisk, beat remaining ½ cup cream until stiff peaks form and fold into salmon mixture. Turn into prepared mold. Refrigerate until well chilled and firm. Unmold onto plate and let sit in refrigerator at least 2 hours before serving. Serve on good dense bread or crackers. Makes 6 to 8 servings.

Turkey Salad Appetizers

From Pat Hatch of West Des Moines, Iowa

¾ cup cooked turkey, chopped
⅓ cup celery, finely chopped
2 tablespoons red bell pepper, finely chopped
2 tablespoons reduced-fat mayonnaise
⅛ teaspoon salt
Dash of pepper

Combine ingredients and mix well. Cover; refrigerate 1 to 2 hours to blend flavors. To serve, spread on sliced vegetables (cucumbers, celery, zucchini, tomatoes), crackers, or cocktail bread slices.

Chicken Wings Mexicali

1 cup vegetable oil
1 cup picante sauce
1 pound tortilla chips

4 pounds chicken wings
2 cups pitted black olives, chopped

Preheat oven to 350 degrees. Whisk together oil and picante sauce. Crush tortilla chips in food processor and put in another bowl. Fold small tips of chicken wings under main wing bone to form triangle. Dip chicken in sauce mixture, then dredge in ground chips until coated. Place on foil-lined baking sheet and sprinkle with chopped olives. Bake 1 hour, until brown and crisp on outside and tender inside. Serve hot. Makes 4 to 6 servings.

Curried Wings

2 pounds chicken wings
1 red bell pepper, chopped
1 small onion, diced
2 cloves garlic, crushed
1 cup plain yogurt
1 tablespoon curry powder

Cut off and discard small tips of chicken wings but don't disjoint wings. Heat large, heavy skillet and, without adding fat, put in wings. Cook, turning, about 10 minutes until chicken has browned lightly in its own natural fat. Add red pepper, onion, and garlic. Continue to cook and stir until onion begins to turn golden brown. Combine yogurt and curry powder and add to skillet. Cover and simmer 1 hour. Makes 2 to 3 servings.

Curry Favor Meatballs

From Jennifer Phelps of Carlisle, Iowa

1 pound ground beef
1 cup quick-cooking rice, uncooked
1 egg, lightly beaten
¾ cup onion, finely chopped

½ teaspoon salt
⅛ teaspoon black pepper
1 tablespoon butter
1 tablespoon vegetable oil
1 (10¾-ounce) can condensed Cheddar cheese soup
1 tablespoon Worcestershire sauce
2 cloves garlic, minced
1 tablespoon curry powder
Dash of cayenne pepper

Thoroughly mix together ground beef, rice, egg, onion, salt, and pepper. Form into small meatballs about 1 inch in diameter. Freeze. (This is an important step because it helps hold the meatballs together.)

Before serving, heat butter and oil together in large skillet. Put frozen meatballs in hot fat and cook until browned. Remove from skillet. Add soup, Worcestershire, garlic, curry powder, and cayenne pepper. Blend well. If sauce is too thick, thin with 1 or 2 tablespoons milk. Return meatballs to sauce. Serve warm. Makes 8 servings.

The main lesson of recipe writing is easy—Never Assume. A chocolate cake recipe that called for half a cup of cocoa prompted one caller to ask if it mattered what kind of "hot chocolate" she used in the cake. Now I always say "cocoa powder" (you know, the dry kind in the dark brown Hershey's can). The same is true of "oatmeal." Call it "rolled oats" if you want the dry ingredients, or someone will call about using a bowl of the prepared cereal. For the same reason, I always spell out tablespoon and teaspoon. Those big T's and little t's can cause lots of problems. It's best to spell out everything.

Swiss Quiche Bites

A favorite "munchable"

2 medium sweet onions, coarsely chopped
2 tablespoons butter or margarine
Pastry for 2-crust pie (see recipe, p. 215)
4 slices bacon, cooked crisp and crumbled
1 cup grated Swiss cheese
3 eggs, beaten
1½ cups half-and-half cream
½ teaspoon salt
Dash of pepper

Preheat oven to 350 degrees. Sauté onions in butter until golden and tender but not brown. Line 4 (5-inch) tart pans with pastry. Divide onions, bacon, and cheese evenly among tarts. Combine eggs, half-and-half, and seasonings. Pour over onion mixture in tart shells. Bake 30 to 35 minutes or until custard is set. Let stand 10 minutes before serving. To serve, cut each tart into 8 wedges. Makes 32 appetizers.

Bruschetta Mozzarella

1 loaf (1 pound) Italian bread
⅓ cup olive oil
1 clove garlic, minced
½ teaspoon salt (optional)
¼ teaspoon coarsely ground black pepper
½ cup green onions, thinly sliced
¾ cup chopped tomatoes
1½ cups (6 ounces) shredded mozzarella cheese
Fresh parsley sprigs (optional)

Preheat oven to 500 degrees. Cut bread in half lengthwise. Place cut sides up on foil-lined baking sheet. Combine oil, garlic, salt, and pepper; drizzle over bread. Sprinkle with onions and tomatoes; top with cheese. Bake in upper half of oven 5 to 7 minutes or until cheese is melted and edges of bread are browned. Cut into 1-inch pieces. Place on serving platter; garnish with parsley, if desired. Makes about 28 appetizers.

Focaccia Squares

1 (16-ounce) package hot roll mix
1¼ cups hot water, heated to 120 to 130 degrees
2 tablespoons olive oil
Cornmeal
1 (10½-ounce) container cheese snack (Neufchâtel cheese with garlic and herbs)
1 large red onion, cut into slivers (about 2 cups)
4 tablespoons Parmesan cheese
½ teaspoon coarsely ground pepper
Fresh basil leaves (optional)

Preheat oven to 400 degrees. Stir together flour mixture and yeast from hot roll mix in large bowl. Add water and olive oil, mixing until dough pulls away from sides of bowl. On floured surface, knead dough 5 minutes or until smooth and elastic. Divide dough into 2 balls. Cover; let stand 10 minutes. On lightly floured surface, roll out each ball into 14 × 6-inch rectangle. Place each rectangle on greased cookie sheet sprinkled with cornmeal.

Mix cheese snack and onion; spread half of mixture evenly over each rectangle. Sprinkle each rectangle with 2 tablespoons Parmesan and ¼ teaspoon pepper.

Bake 10 to 20 minutes or until edges are golden brown. Cool 10 minutes; cut into 2-inch squares. Garnish each with basil leaves, if desired. Makes about 42 appetizers.

Garden Pizza Squares

Often called vegetable pizza

2 (8-ounce) packages refrigerated crescent rolls
1 (8-ounce) package cream cheese, softened
1 (3-ounce) package cream cheese, softened
⅓ cup ranch salad dressing
1 teaspoon dried dillweed, crushed
3 cups chopped fresh vegetables (tomatoes, green peppers, black olives, green onions, carrots)
1 cup shredded Cheddar, mozzarella, or Monterey Jack cheese (optional)

To make crust, unroll crescent rolls and pat into 15 × 10-inch jelly roll pan. Bake according to package directions. Cool. Meanwhile, in medium bowl, combine cream cheese, salad dressing, and dill. Spread over cooled crust. Arrange chopped vegetables over cream cheese mixture. Sprinkle shredded cheese over vegetables, if desired. Cut into small squares for serving. Makes about 36 servings.

Directions always say how many servings should be expected to come from a recipe. It's only a guess, of course. Are you serving husky high school football players with mammoth appetites or eighty-year-old grandmothers who eat like baby birds? A general rule of thumb could be this: it makes four servings if they like it and six or eight if they don't.

Pizza Bagels

½ cup chunk-style spaghetti sauce or pizza sauce
2 bagels, cut in half horizontally
4 pinches oregano
24 pepperoni slices
1 cup shredded mozzarella cheese

Put ⅛ cup spaghetti or pizza sauce on each bagel half. Sprinkle pinch of oregano on sauce and top each bagel half with 6 pepperoni slices and ¼ cup mozzarella cheese. (You can freeze these at this point.)

To serve, preheat oven to 375 degrees. Bake on foil-lined cookie sheet 8 to 10 minutes or until cheese bubbles and begins to brown. Allow extra cooking time if frozen.

Use any of your favorite pizza toppings: sliced olives, cooked mushrooms, sautéed green pepper, and onion. Makes 4 servings.

Quick Pizza Puffs

Make in a jiffy

1 (10-ounce) tube refrigerated biscuits
Oregano or Italian seasoning
Garlic powder
5 ounces mozzarella cheese, cut into 10 (1-inch) square cubes
1 to 2 tablespoons prepared pizza or spaghetti sauce

Lightly spray cookie sheet with cooking spray; set aside. Separate dough into 10 pieces. Make indentation in center of each biscuit piece with thumb. Lightly sprinkle indentation with oregano and garlic powder; top with 2 cheese cubes. Pull dough over cheese and firmly pinch together so cheese is completely enclosed to prevent it from oozing out during baking. Place on prepared cookie sheet, seam-side down. Repeat with remaining biscuits, seasonings, and cheese, placing them on sheet 2 inches apart. Lightly brush tops of puffs with pizza or spaghetti sauce.

Preheat oven to 375 degrees. Refrigerate puffs 15 minutes, then remove to oven and bake until golden, 10 to 12 minutes. Serve warm. Makes 10 puffs.

NOTE: To reheat, loosely wrap 1 baked puff in paper towel. Microwave on high until warm, about 25 seconds.

Cucumber Sandwiches

See Tea Party for Twelve, p. 249.

Radish Sandwiches

See Tea Party for Twelve, p. 249.

Salmon Spread Sandwiches

See Tea Party for Twelve, p. 250.

Artichoke Rumakis

See Elegant Dinner for Eight, p. 242.

Stuffed Peapods

See Champagne Brunch for Twenty-four, p. 234.

Oriental Munchies

¼ cup bottled teriyaki sauce
1½ tablespoons vegetable oil
2 teaspoons sugar
¼ teaspoon ground ginger
1½ cups whole natural almonds
1½ cups walnut halves or pieces
¾ cup raw sunflower kernels
3 cups toasted oat cereal (such as Cheerios)
1 cup (2½ ounces) banana chips
¾ cup seedless raisins

Preheat oven to 250 degrees. Blend teriyaki sauce, oil, sugar, and ginger in large bowl until sugar dissolves; stir in almonds and walnuts until thoroughly coated. Let stand 20 minutes; stir occasionally. Stir in sunflower kernels until coated. Add cereal, tossing to combine.

Turn out on large shallow baking pan or cookie sheet, spreading mixture evenly. Bake 15 minutes. Remove from oven; stir gently. Return to oven and bake 15 minutes longer. Remove pan to wire rack and cool completely. Stir in banana chips and raisins. Store in tightly covered container. Makes 7 cups.

Puppy Chow Snack Mix

From Jeffrey Charlson of LeMars, Iowa

½ cup margarine
1 cup chunky peanut butter
1 (12-ounce) package semisweet chocolate chips
1 (24-ounce) box Crispix cereal
2 cups powdered sugar

Melt margarine, peanut butter, and chocolate chips in double boiler. Pour melted mixture over cereal in large bowl. Stir well to coat cereal. Place coated cereal in a large brown-paper bag; shake well. Add powdered sugar to cereal in bag; shake well to coat cereal. Store in airtight container in refrigerator.

Consommé Ridgeway

See Elegant Dinner for Eight, p. 242.

Cauliflower-Cheddar Soup

From Julie Trusler of J.T.'s Cuisine, Newton, Iowa

½ cup green onions (including some of the green tops), sliced
2 tablespoons butter
3 cups cauliflower florets
3 cups chicken broth
8 ounces sharp Cheddar cheese spread (Mertz or Woody's) or sharp Cheddar cheese
Green scallion tops, sliced, for garnish

In heavy saucepan, cook green onions in butter over moderate heat until soft. Add cauliflower and broth. Bring liquid to boil and simmer, covered, 12 to 15 minutes or until cauliflower is very tender. Puree mixture in batches and return to pan. Add cheese spread and stir until melted. If soup is too thick, add some milk or cream. Heat over moderate heat until mixture is hot. Top each serving with sprinkle of sliced scallion tops. Makes 4 or 5 servings.

Creamy Broccoli Soup

½ cup water
1 (10-ounce) package frozen chopped broccoli, thawed and drained
1 medium onion, chopped (about ½ cup)
1 large stalk celery, chopped (about ½ cup)
2 tablespoons butter or margarine
2 tablespoons flour
1 (14½-ounce) can chicken broth
⅛ teaspoon pepper
Dash of ground nutmeg

7 slices American cheese product, torn into 1-inch pieces
1 cup nonfat plain yogurt

Heat water to boiling in 3-quart saucepan. Add broccoli, onion, and celery. Cover and return to boil. Boil 5 minutes or until broccoli is tender. Do not drain. Transfer broccoli mixture to bowl. Heat butter in 3-quart saucepan over medium heat until melted. Stir in flour. Cook, stirring constantly, until mixture is smooth and bubbly; remove from heat. Stir in chicken broth. Heat to boiling, stirring constantly. Boil and stir 1 minute. Stir in broccoli mixture, pepper, and nutmeg. Stir in cheese. Heat over low heat, stirring occasionally, just until cheese is melted; remove from heat. Mix ½ cup soup and yogurt in small bowl; stir into remaining soup. Makes 4 servings.

Cream of Carrot Soup

From Nancy Catena of San Francisco
People will swear this is the best cheese soup they ever tasted

6 tablespoons butter
½ cup chopped onion
2 cups sliced carrots
1 teaspoon salt
3 chicken bouillon cubes
3 cups boiling water
¼ cup uncooked rice
2 cups milk
Sour cream and fresh dill, for garnish

Heat butter in saucepan; add onions and sauté until lightly brown. Add carrots and salt, tossing to coat with butter. Cook, tightly covered, over low heat 20 minutes, stirring occasionally. Add bouillon cubes, water, and rice and simmer, covered, 1 hour, stirring occasionally to prevent burning. Pour ingredients into blender or food processor and blend until smooth. Return to saucepan and add milk. Heat and serve with dollop of sour cream and sprinkle of chopped fresh dill. Makes about 1¼ quarts.

NOTE: This freezes well. Soup is also good without the 2 cups milk.

French Tomato Soup

From Jennifer Phelps of Carlisle, Iowa

3 cups diced potatoes
1 clove garlic, minced
½ teaspoon seasoned salt
2 cups New York extra-sharp Cheddar cheese, shredded
1 quart whole milk
½ cup half-and-half cream
1 (28-ounce) can Italian tomatoes with basil

Cook potatoes in water to cover until very tender and most of liquid is absorbed. Mash potatoes with potato masher. Add garlic, seasoned salt, and cheese. Cook until cheese is melted and mixture is smooth. Add milk and half-and-half. Continue heating until soup is hot but not boiling. Put tomatoes through sieve; discard pulp and seeds. Add tomato puree slowly to soup, stirring constantly. Continue heating until soup is hot enough to serve. Do not boil. Makes 8 servings.

NOTE: Do not substitute skim, 1 percent, or 2 percent milk for whole milk or soup will curdle.

Healthful Beef-Noodle Soup

Good—and good for you

8 cups water
1 tablespoon beef bouillon granules
2 teaspoons no-salt seasoning blend
½ teaspoon onion powder
½ teaspoon garlic powder
⅓ (4-ounce) package cholesterol-free noodles
2 cups frozen mixed vegetables
1 pound boneless beef sirloin, cut into ½-inch cubes

Bring water, bouillon, seasoning blend, onion powder, and garlic powder to boil in Dutch oven or stock pot. Stir in noodles and vegetables. Return to boil and cook 10 to 12 minutes or until noodles are tender.

Meanwhile, coat large skillet with cooking spray. Cook beef cubes in skillet over medium heat, stirring frequently, just until cooked through, about 3 minutes. Add to cooked noodles mixture and heat through. Makes 6 servings.

Fresh Gazpacho

A garden delight

1 cucumber
2 medium tomatoes, cored and quartered
½ medium onion
2 stalks celery, with strings removed
2 carrots, peeled and trimmed
1 red bell pepper, cored and seeds removed
1 green bell pepper, cored and seeds removed
2¼ cups tomato-based vegetable juice
1 tablespoon lime juice
1 tablespoon balsamic vinegar
1 teaspoon ground cumin
2 tablespoons fresh cilantro leaves or chopped parsley

Puree vegetables individually in food processor. Put puree in large bowl; add juices, vinegar, and cumin. Stir together. Add cilantro or parsley. Cover and refrigerate. Serve chilled with croutons. Makes 1 quart or 6 servings.

Norwegian Curried Cranberry Soup

From Mimi Gormezano of Iowa City, Iowa

4 cups chicken stock
2 cups fresh or frozen cranberries, washed
1 medium onion, finely chopped
¼ cup sugar
1¾ cups half-and-half cream
1 to 2 tablespoons curry powder

1 tablespoon cornstarch
1 teaspoon salt
Pinch of cayenne pepper, to taste
1 tablespoon fresh lemon juice
½ cup toasted shredded coconut, for garnish

In saucepan, put stock, cranberries, onion, and sugar and cook until mixture comes to boil. Simmer 5 or 6 minutes or until about a quarter of the cranberries have burst. In small bowl, mix half-and-half, curry powder, cornstarch, salt, and cayenne until smooth. Stir into soup. Simmer until mixture thickens but do not boil. Remove from heat and add lemon juice. Puree in blender or processor. Refrigerate until cold. Garnish with toasted coconut. Makes 6 servings.

Strawberry Soup

A summer specialty

2 cups strawberries, cold
1 cup reduced-fat buttermilk
1 tablespoon plus 1 teaspoon sugar
Mint leaves for garnish (optional)

In food processor or blender, blend all ingredients. Serve immediately or chill in refrigerator. Garnish with mint leaves, if desired. Makes 4 servings.

VARIATION: Substitute raspberries, cantaloupe, honeydew melon, or nectarines for strawberries.

Tortilla-Cheese Soup

A family pleaser

1 (5¼-ounce) package dry au gratin potatoes
1 (15¼-ounce) can whole kernel corn, undrained
1 cup picante sauce
2 cups water

2 cups milk
1½ cups shredded cheese for tacos
1 (2¼-ounce) can sliced ripe olives, drained

In large saucepan, combine potatoes, corn, picante sauce, and water. Bring to boil; reduce heat. Cover and simmer 25 minutes or until potatoes are tender, stirring occasionally. Add milk, cheese, and olives. Cook until cheese is melted and soup is heated through, stirring occasionally. Serve with tortilla chips. Makes about 8 cups or 6 servings.

Wild Rice Soup

From Gerie Benson of West Des Moines, Iowa

4 cups water
1 cup wild rice
3 carrots, sliced thin or grated
3 stalks celery, finely chopped
¼ cup onion, chopped
1 pound ham, cubed
½ pound bacon, cooked crisp and crumbled
1 can cream of mushroom soup
1 can cream of chicken soup
1 (14½-ounce) can chicken broth
1 cup half-and-half cream
Pepper (optional)
Paprika (optional)
Garlic powder (optional)

Boil water and pour over wild rice. Set aside 15 minutes, then bring to boil and add remaining ingredients to wild rice mixture. Reduce heat and simmer 3 to 4 hours. Makes about 8 servings.

Apple-Mint Tea

Refreshing on a hot day

2 quarts cold water
6 tea bags
1 teaspoon chopped fresh mint leaves
1 (12-ounce) container frozen apple juice concentrate, thawed
½ cup bottled lemon juice or bottled lime juice
½ cup sugar

In large saucepan, bring water to boil. Pour into heat-proof pitcher or bowl; add tea bags and mint. Cover; steep 4 minutes. Remove tea bags; add remaining ingredients. Stir until sugar dissolves. Serve over ice. Makes about 2 quarts.

Brunch Punch

Citrus picker-upper

2 scoops lemonade drink mix
1 quart orange juice
2 cups club soda

Stir drink mix and orange juice in pitcher until mix is dissolved. Just before serving, add club soda. Serve over ice. Makes 6 (1-cup) servings.

Cinnamon Coffee

Perfect on a dreary day

3 tablespoons instant nonfat dry milk
2½ tablespoons freeze-dried coffee
2 tablespoons sugar
½ teaspoon cinnamon
Pinch of ground cloves

Mix all ingredients in jar. For each serving, add 2 teaspoons mix to 6 ounces boiling water. Makes 12 servings.

Grown-Up Hot Chocolate

Soothing and warm

3 tablespoons sugar
2 tablespoons unsweetened cocoa powder
1¾ cups milk, divided

Combine sugar and cocoa powder in small saucepan with wire whisk. Add ¼ cup milk. Whisk over medium heat until smooth. Add remaining milk; heat until hot, whisking occasionally. Makes 2 (8-ounce) cups.

VARIATIONS
Hot Chocolate Cherry Cordial: Whisk in 1½ tablespoons kirsch (cherry-flavored brandy) just before serving. Garnish with whipped cream and maraschino cherry, if desired.
Mexican Hot Chocolate: Add ½ teaspoon ground cinnamon to sugar-chocolate mixture; proceed with recipe. Garnish with cinnamon stick, if desired.
Orange-Spice Cocoa: Add ¼ teaspoon ground nutmeg to sugar-chocolate mixture; proceed with recipe. Stir in 1½ tablespoons orange-flavored liqueur just before serving. Garnish with orange twist or slice, if desired.
Mocha Sensation: Add 1 tablespoon instant freeze-dried coffee when stirring in remaining milk. Stir in 1½ tablespoons coffee-flavored liqueur just before serving. Garnish with whipped cream and chocolate curls or chocolate sprinkles, if desired.

Hot Apple Harvest Tea

1½ cups water
½ cup apple juice
3 whole cloves or dash of ground cloves

1 cinnamon stick or ⅛ teaspoon ground cinnamon
1 tablespoon instant tea mix

Bring water, apple juice, and spices to boil in medium saucepan. Remove cloves and cinnamon stick. Add iced tea mix; stir to dissolve. Serve hot. Makes 2 (1-cup) servings.

Hot Cranberry Punch

See Holiday Dinner, p. 261.

Irish Coffee

4 ounces hot coffee
1 or 2 teaspoons brown sugar
1½ ounces Irish whiskey
Lightly whipped cream

Preheat Irish coffee glass with hot water. Allow to stand for several seconds, then empty. Fill warmed glass with coffee; add sugar and stir to dissolve. Add Irish whiskey and stir. Pour lightly whipped cream over back of spoon so cream floats on top. Do not stir. Sip hot coffee and whiskey through the cream. Makes 1 serving.

Over the years Iowa cooks and readers of the *Register* have seen many changes come to their kitchens. Prepared foods, convenient mixes, and take-out entrees have changed the way dinner is put together. And whatever happened to Sunday dinner in many Iowa homes? Kitchen counters and cabinets are full of items that weren't there twenty years ago—microwave ovens, convection ovens, food processors, bread machines, and espresso coffee machines. And Grandma likely would chuckle. One process that she got rid of—grinding coffee beans—is now trendy again.

Mulled Cider

An autumn favorite

1½ cups brown sugar
1 teaspoon whole allspice
1 teaspoon whole cloves
¼ teaspoon salt
1 cinnamon stick
¼ teaspoon ground nutmeg
6 cups apple cider or apple juice

Heat over low heat for 20 minutes. Strain into large bowl. Serve with dollops of whipped cream, if desired. Makes 12 (½-cup) servings.

Simple Syrup

1 cup water
2 cups sugar

Combine in saucepan. Heat and stir until sugar is dissolved. Cool. Pour into glass jar or plastic container. Cover and refrigerate. Use as a sweetener for summer drinks.

Lemonade

4 cups water
1 cup Simple Syrup
1⅓ cups fresh lemon juice

Mix ingredients thoroughly and chill.

Tea Fruit Punch

2½ cups boiling water
6 tea bags or 6 teaspoons loose tea
¼ teaspoon ground allspice
¼ teaspoon ground cinnamon
¼ teaspoon ground nutmeg
¾ cup sugar
1 pint cranberry juice, chilled
1 (12-ounce) can ginger ale, chilled
1 cup orange juice, chilled
½ cup fresh lemon juice, chilled

Pour boiling water over tea and spices; cover and steep 5 minutes. Strain tea and stir in sugar. Let cool. Combine tea base with remaining chilled liquids. Pour over ice and serve. Makes 6 to 8 servings.

Greens & More

Spinach Salad

From Evelyn Carlson of Des Moines, Iowa

2 hard-cooked eggs
1 pound bacon, cooked crisp and crumbled
4 quarts fresh spinach, torn into bite-sized pieces

DRESSING
⅔ cup salad oil
¼ cup wine vinegar
2 tablespoons red wine
2 teaspoons soy sauce
1 teaspoon sugar
1 teaspoon dry mustard
¼ teaspoon curry powder
½ teaspoon salt
½ teaspoon garlic salt
1 teaspoon freshly ground black pepper

Chop eggs; mix bacon with spinach and chopped eggs in large bowl. Combine dressing ingredients. Pour dressing over spinach and toss. Makes 8 to 10 servings.

In the late *Des Moines Tribune,* I had a syndicated question-answer column for six years called "Let's Ask the Cook." People wrote in questions, and I attempted to answer them. In about 90 percent of the cases, readers wanted old recipes, treasured bits of their family histories. Gooseberry pie like Aunt Margaret used to make, tomato soup spice cake, or homemade marshmallows. Grandmas, moms, and aunts usually kept those secrets in their heads. That's why old terms such as "pinch of this" and "dash of that" are still around, even though they are frustrating to many contemporary cooks, who only feel comfortable with exact measures.

Elegant Spinach Salad

From Mary Upton of Des Moines, Iowa

1 bunch fresh spinach, torn into bite-sized pieces
1 (11-ounce) can mandarin oranges, drained
½ pound fresh mushrooms, sliced
1 cup bean sprouts
1 (8-ounce) can water chestnuts, drained and sliced
½ cup green onions, julienned

DRESSING
½ cup salad oil
½ cup soy sauce
2 tablespoons lemon juice
1½ tablespoons onion flakes
½ teaspoon honey
½ teaspoon pepper

Combine salad ingredients in large bowl. In small bowl, blend dressing ingredients. Toss salad lightly with dressing and serve. Makes 6 servings.

Popeye and Olive Oyl Apple Salad

From Jennifer Phelps of Carlisle, Iowa

1 bunch fresh spinach, cleaned and dried
1 red apple, unpeeled, cored and thinly sliced
½ cup toasted walnuts, for garnish

DRESSING
3 tablespoons balsamic vinegar
½ cup olive oil
1 tablespoon sugar
1 clove garlic, minced
1 teaspoon salt

Toss salad ingredients, except walnuts, together in bowl. Mix dressing ingredients with wire whisk until sugar dissolves and dressing is well blended. Pour over salad. Garnish with walnuts. Makes 4 servings.

Endive Salad

2 Belgian endives, washed and dried
4 mushrooms, cleaned
1 unpeeled apple
Half of sweet yellow bell pepper, cut into strips
2 tablespoons chopped walnuts

DRESSING
4 tablespoons mayonnaise
Salt
Freshly ground black pepper
1 lemon
1 tablespoon balsamic vinegar

Slice endives lengthwise into salad bowl. Coarsely chop mushrooms and apple and add to endive. Add pepper strips. Combine mayonnaise, salt, pepper, juice of lemon, and balsamic vinegar to make dressing. Pour dressing over salad, add walnuts, and toss gently. Makes 2 servings.

Mandarin Orange Salad

From Deborah Cave of Des Moines, Iowa

1 cup sliced almonds
2 tablespoons sugar
¼ head leaf lettuce
¼ head romaine lettuce
2 stalks celery, sliced
2 green onions, chopped
1 (11-ounce) can mandarin oranges, drained

DRESSING
¼ cup vegetable oil
2 tablespoons sugar
2 tablespoons vinegar
1 teaspoon fresh parsley, chopped
Dash of pepper
Dash of Tabasco sauce

Cook almonds in 2 tablespoons sugar, stirring constantly until sugar melts. Cool and reserve. Tear lettuce into bite-sized pieces and combine with celery and green onions. Combine dressing ingredients and mix until sugar dissolves. Just before serving, add almonds and mandarin orange slices to greens, pour dressing over all, and toss. Makes 4 servings.

Orange-Onion Salad

See Holiday Dinner, p. 268.

Hearts of Palm Salad

See Elegant Dinner for Eight, p. 243.

Apple Coleslaw

1 small head green cabbage, shredded
2 crisp eating apples, cored and thinly sliced
1 carrot, grated
1 small red bell pepper, chopped
1 small green bell pepper, chopped
½ small onion, chopped

DRESSING
½ cup nonfat plain yogurt
½ cup reduced-fat buttermilk
1½ teaspoons sugar
1 teaspoon prepared horseradish
½ teaspoon celery seeds
¼ teaspoon salt

Mix salad ingredients together. Thoroughly blend dressing ingredients and pour over salad. Makes 6 to 8 servings.

Cabbage Salad

1 head cabbage
1 small onion
½ green bell pepper
1 carrot
1 teaspoon celery salt

DRESSING
¾ cup vinegar
¾ cup vegetable oil
1 cup sugar

Chop cabbage, onion, pepper, and carrot. Stir in celery salt. In saucepan, bring dressing ingredients to simmer and stir until sugar is dissolved. Pour over salad ingredients. Cover tightly and refrigerate 24 hours. Keeps well for several days. Makes 8 servings.

Citrus Slaw

1 small head cabbage, cut in long, thin shreds (9 to 10 cups)
1 small green bell pepper, finely chopped
¼ cup thinly sliced green onions
3 oranges, peeled, cut into bite-sized pieces, well drained
Green pepper rings and orange cartwheel slices, for garnish (optional)

DRESSING
½ cup mayonnaise or salad dressing
Grated peel of 1 orange
2 tablespoons freshly squeezed orange juice
1 tablespoon sugar
¼ teaspoon salt
Pepper

In large bowl, combine salad ingredients; chill. Combine dressing ingredients. To serve, toss salad with dressing. Garnish with green pepper rings and orange cartwheel slices, if desired. Makes about 9 cups or 6 to 8 servings.

Sweet 'n' Sour Fruit Slaw

From Judith Anderson of Madrid, Iowa

1 head cabbage, shredded
1 medium apple, chopped
1 cup green grapes
1 (11-ounce) can mandarin oranges, drained
¼ cup raisins
1 cup celery, chopped

DRESSING
1 cup cream-style cottage cheese
¼ cup milk
3 tablespoons lemon juice

2 tablespoons vegetable oil
2 tablespoons honey

In mixing bowl, combine salad ingredients. Put dressing ingredients in blender and mix thoroughly. Pour dressing over salad mixture and toss. Makes 8 servings.

Spiced Red Cabbage

From the Strawtown Inn, Pella, Iowa

1 large head red cabbage, very finely sliced (about 5 cups)
1 cup chopped, unpeeled, crisp tart apples (such as Jonathan, Winesap, or McIntosh)
1 tablespoon whole allspice
½ teaspoon salt
¼ teaspoon grated nutmeg
¼ teaspoon ground cinnamon
¼ teaspoon freshly ground black pepper
¼ cup red wine vinegar
⅓ cup brown sugar
2 tablespoons butter (or more, as desired)

Place cabbage in large sauté pan and add enough water to cover. Bring to boil; lower heat and simmer, covered, until cabbage is limp and soft, about 5 minutes. Drain off all but ½ cup water. Add apples; toss and continue cooking until apples are tender, about 15 minutes. Add spices, vinegar, and brown sugar and continue cooking until cabbage and apple mixture is tender and most of liquid is gone. Add butter and serve. Makes 6 servings.

Cabbage 'n' Macaroni Slaw

1½ cups thinly sliced red cabbage
2 cups cooked elbow macaroni
2 cups chopped, seeded cucumber
¼ cup sliced celery

¼ cup sliced green onions and tops
12 cherry tomatoes, cut into quarters

DRESSING
½ cup reduced-fat mayonnaise or salad dressing
¼ cup reduced-fat sour cream
3 to 4 teaspoons Dijon-style mustard
2 teaspoons lemon juice
1 teaspoon white wine vinegar
2 tablespoons fresh parsley, chopped
1½ teaspoons dried dillweed
¼ teaspoon salt
¼ teaspoon white pepper

Combine salad ingredients in large glass bowl. Combine dressing ingredients; spoon over macaroni mixture and toss. Cover with plastic wrap and refrigerate several hours to allow flavors to blend. Makes about 12 servings.

More than a decade ago the newspaper did a "Cooking of Iowa" series, showing the diversity of simple and elegant, old and new, when it comes to food in the Hawkeye State. One of the most interesting features focused on Iowa's historic homes. From Terrace Hill in Des Moines, home of Iowa's governor, to the General Dodge House in Council Bluffs and George Wyth House in Waterloo, the parties held there were fascinating to recount. Included in the series were recipes from an era when there were no supermarkets to run to. Planners of elegant soirees used vegetables and fruits from gardens and orchards and raised chickens, cattle, and hogs for main dishes. They even grew flowers for the centerpieces. The old recipes with "hot" and "moderate" oven temperatures, along with household hints sprinkled through cookbooks from the historic homes, showed just how resourceful Iowans had to be back then.

Caesar Chicken Salad

Carbo-loaded main-dish salad

2 cups chicken-flavor stuffing mix
½ cup hot water
1½ cups cooked chicken strips
1 small red bell pepper, cut into thin strips
⅔ cup prepared Caesar or Italian salad dressing, divided
3 cups torn romaine lettuce
½ cup Parmesan cheese, shredded

Stir stuffing mix and hot water together in large bowl just to moisten. Let stand 5 minutes. Stir chicken and pepper strips into stuffing mixture. Add ⅓ cup dressing; toss lightly. Cover. Refrigerate until ready to serve. Toss with lettuce and remaining ⅓ cup dressing just before serving. Sprinkle with cheese. Makes 4 servings.

Garden Bounty Chicken Salad

From Bonnie Lasater of Des Moines, Iowa

2 cups cauliflower florets
½ cup carrots, sliced
6 cups spinach
1 cup celery, sliced
⅓ cup green bell pepper, chopped
2 tablespoons green onion, chopped
2 cups cooked chicken, diced
2 small tomatoes, cut into wedges
1 cup Swiss cheese, shredded

DRESSING
¾ cup sour cream
⅓ cup plain yogurt
½ cup grated cucumber
½ teaspoon garlic salt

In covered saucepan, cook cauliflower and carrots until crisp-tender (3 to 5 minutes). Drain. In large bowl, layer 3 cups spinach, cauliflower, carrots, celery, pepper, green onions, chicken, tomato wedges, remaining 3 cups spinach, and cheese. Mix dressing ingredients and pour over salad. Allow to sit at least 2 hours. Makes 6 servings.

Turkey-Melon Salad

¾ pound deli smoked turkey breast, cut into ¼-inch pieces
¾ pound cantaloupe, cut into cubes or balls
1 cup chopped celery
½ cup green onion, thinly sliced

DRESSING
2 tablespoons chutney, chopped
2 tablespoons olive oil
1 tablespoon white wine vinegar
½ tablespoon Dijon-style mustard
½ tablespoon reduced-sodium soy sauce
⅛ teaspoon red pepper flakes
1 large garlic clove, minced

In large bowl combine turkey, cantaloupe, celery, and green onions. In small bowl, whisk together dressing ingredients. Combine dressing with turkey mixture. Cover and refrigerate 1 hour. Serve on greens, if desired. Makes 6 servings.

Shrimp-Yogurt Salad

From Shelene Springer of Guthrie Center, Iowa

1 cup bean sprouts
½ cup mushrooms, sliced
1 cup cherry tomatoes, cut in half
1 can shrimp
½ cup diced avocado

½ cup sliced cucumber or zucchini
Torn spinach and lettuce
Slivered almonds and 1 (11-ounce) can mandarin oranges, well drained, for garnish

DRESSING
8 ounces plain yogurt
3 tablespoons honey
2 teaspoons lemon juice
⅓ cup half-and-half cream or milk
Salt, pepper, cinnamon, and ground cloves to taste

Put bean sprouts, mushrooms, tomatoes, shrimp, avocado, cucumber, and spinach and lettuce in large bowl and toss lightly. Mix dressing ingredients. Toss with salad ingredients. Garnish with slivered almonds and mandarin oranges.

Pasta–Black Bean Salad

1 pound dried pasta (such as penne or rotelli)
1 (15-ounce) can black beans
1 red or yellow bell pepper, cored, seeded, and chopped
¼ cup chopped and drained oil-packed sun-dried tomatoes
4 ounces fresh mozzarella cheese, cut into ½-inch dice
1 bunch green onions, trimmed and thinly sliced (include green tops)
Yellow bell pepper, thinly sliced (optional)

DRESSING
2 tablespoons fresh cilantro, minced
1 tablespoon fresh thyme leaves, minced
3 tablespoons fresh basil leaves, minced
2 medium garlic cloves, minced
2 tablespoons white wine vinegar
1 tablespoon balsamic vinegar
¾ cup olive oil
Salt and pepper to taste

Cook pasta just to al dente in boiling water. Drain and place in large bowl.

DRESSING: Combine cilantro, thyme, basil, garlic, and vinegars. Drizzle in oil, stirring constantly. Add salt and pepper to taste.

ASSEMBLY: Pour dressing over pasta and toss. Place black beans in small strainer; rinse under cold water. Drain. When pasta is cool, add black beans, bell pepper, tomatoes, and cheese. Taste salad; add more salt and pepper if necessary. If salad needs more oil, drizzle on a little from tomatoes and toss. Refrigerate. May be made 2 days ahead of serving. Before serving, toss with onions. Garnish with thin slices of yellow bell pepper, if desired. Makes 8 servings.

PEO Pasta Salad

From Garnishes Catering, Urbandale, Iowa

SALAD
12 ounces fettuccine
1½ pounds broccoli florets
2 medium zucchini, thinly sliced
6 green onions, sliced
1 sweet red bell pepper, sliced
1 (6-ounce) can sliced black olives
⅔ cup grated Parmesan cheese
½ teaspoon salt
½ teaspoon pepper
Lettuce leaves
2 cups cherry tomatoes, halved, for garnish

SAUCE
¼ cup chopped fresh basil
1 clove garlic
2 eggs
½ teaspoon dry mustard
½ teaspoon salt
½ teaspoon lemon juice
1 tablespoon wine vinegar

1½ cups oil
½ cup sour cream

SALAD: Cook fettuccine according to package directions; drain. Add vegetables, olives, cheese, salt, and pepper. Toss and chill.

SAUCE: Blend basil and garlic in blender 30 seconds. Add eggs, dry mustard, salt, lemon juice, and vinegar; blend. Slowly add oil and blend. Add sour cream and blend 5 seconds.

If desired, add chunks of turkey breast to salad.

To serve, toss salad with basil sauce. Serve on lettuce leaves and garnish with tomato halves. Makes 12 servings.

Walnut-Pasta Vinaigrette

½ cup walnuts, chopped in large pieces
4 ounces vermicelli or spaghetti, broken
2 (6-ounce) jars marinated artichoke hearts, drained and chopped
1 cup sliced fresh mushrooms
2 tomatoes, peeled, seeded, and chopped
2 tablespoons fresh parsley, chopped

DRESSING
¼ cup salad oil
¼ cup red wine vinegar
1 clove garlic, minced
½ teaspoon dried basil leaves, crumbled
Dash of pepper

Toast walnuts at 350 degrees for 5 to 10 minutes; watch carefully to see they don't burn. Set aside. Cook pasta in boiling salted water according to package directions. Rinse and drain. Toss together pasta, artichokes, and mushrooms. In screw-top jar, combine dressing ingredients; shake well. Pour dressing over pasta mixture, tossing to coat. Cover and chill. To serve, add tomatoes, parsley, and walnuts; toss. Serve in lettuce-lined bowl, if desired. Makes 6 servings.

Potato Salad

From Ronda Magnusson of Hartford, Iowa

5 medium potatoes, boiled and peeled
1 small onion, chopped
1 tablespoon sweet red bell pepper, finely chopped
4 sweet pickles, diced
2 hard-cooked eggs, diced

DRESSING
½ cup salad dressing (such as Miracle Whip)
1 teaspoon prepared yellow mustard
1 tablespoon Dijon-style mustard
2 teaspoons celery seeds
1 tablespoon dillweed
3 teaspoons sugar
1 tablespoon sweet pickle juice

Stir together salad ingredients. Mix dressing ingredients and pour over potato mixture. Chill.

Blue Ribbon Potato Salad

Attractive and tasty with tomatoes

5 medium potatoes, peeled or unpeeled
¼ cup olive oil
¼ cup lemon juice
¼ cup fresh parsley, chopped
2 cloves garlic, minced
1 teaspoon salt
1 teaspoon paprika
1 teaspoon ground cumin
2 medium tomatoes, cut into ¾-inch cubes
¾ cup thinly sliced red onion

In heavy 3-quart saucepan, cook potatoes, covered, in 2 inches boiling water 10 to 12 minutes, until just tender. Meanwhile, in large bowl, whisk oil, lemon juice, parsley, garlic, salt, paprika, and cumin. Mix in tomatoes and onion. Drain potatoes thoroughly and add to bowl. Toss gently to coat completely. Serve warm or at room temperature. Makes 4 to 6 servings.

French Potato Salad

From Eliot Nusbaum of Carlisle, Iowa

4 to 6 medium red potatoes
2 (10-ounce) packages frozen French-style green beans
Italian vinaigrette

Cut scrubbed red potatoes in halves or quarters but do not peel. Boil in water to cover until tender but still firm. Drain and cool. Cook green beans in potato water. Drain and cool with potatoes. Moisten potatoes and beans with vinaigrette and allow to stand 1 to 2 hours before serving. Best served slightly warm. Makes 6 servings.

Baked German Potato Salad

For a twist on tradition

2 quarts boiled red potatoes, peeled and sliced

DRESSING
6 slices bacon, crisp-cooked
1 cup celery, finely chopped
1 cup onion, finely chopped
1 tablespoon cornstarch
½ teaspoon salt
½ teaspoon pepper
⅔ cup sugar
⅔ cup cider vinegar
1½ cups water
⅓ cup chopped fresh parsley
2 teaspoons celery seeds

Preheat oven to 375 degrees. Place potatoes in greased 13 × 9-inch baking dish. Set aside. Cook bacon until crisp; crumble and set aside. Reserve fat in skillet. If necessary, add additional fat or oil to make ¼ cup. Stir in celery and onion. Add cornstarch, salt, and pepper and cook 2 minutes. Add sugar, vinegar, and water and stir with whisk. Bring to boil and cook 1 minute. Add parsley, celery seeds, and reserved bacon and combine; remove from heat.

Pour warm dressing over potatoes in baking dish. Mix gently. Bake 45 minutes. Makes 10 to 12 servings.

Potato-Asparagus Salad

1 pound red potatoes, chopped
½ pound asparagus, cut into 2-inch pieces
Lemon Vinaigrette (see recipe, p. 54)

In 2-quart saucepan, place potatoes and enough water to cover; bring to boil. Reduce heat to low; cover and simmer 15 minutes or until potatoes are almost tender. Add asparagus; cook 2 minutes longer or until vegetables are tender. Drain. In large bowl, toss potatoes and asparagus with Lemon Vinaigrette. Serve warm or refrigerate to serve later. Makes 4 servings.

Three-Bean Salad

1 (14½-ounce) can wax beans, drained
1 (15½-ounce) can green beans, drained
1 (15-ounce) can kidney beans, drained
1 cup celery, diced
⅔ cup sweet pickle relish
2 tablespoons sliced pimientos
1 cup prepared ranch dressing

Combine all ingredients, except salad dressing. Toss gently. Add salad dressing and mix well. Makes 4 to 6 servings.

Carrot-Bean Salad

From Karen Brown of Des Moines, Iowa

5 cups cooked carrots
1 bell pepper, chopped
1 onion, sliced
1 cup celery, sliced
1 (15-ounce) can kidney beans
1 cup sugar
½ cup salad oil
¾ cup vinegar
1 tablespoon Worcestershire sauce
1 teaspoon salt
1 teaspoon pepper

1 teaspoon dry or prepared mustard
1 (10¾-ounce) can tomato soup

Mix ingredients and let sit several hours. This should marinate for some time or it will be too sweet. Makes 8 to 10 servings.

Dilled Vegetables

From Dorothy McCoy of Des Moines, Iowa

1 head cauliflower
1 bunch broccoli
8 tablespoons salad oil
1 teaspoon sugar
½ cup wine vinegar
1 teaspoon garlic powder
1 tablespoon dill seeds
1 teaspoon pepper
3 teaspoons salt
2 tablespoons meat tenderizer

Break cauliflower and broccoli into small florets. Mix remaining ingredients and pour over vegetables. Allow to stand 24 hours. Makes about 10 servings.

Gingered Tomatoes

¼ cup white wine vinegar
3 to 4 tablespoons sugar
3 slices fresh ginger, slivered
⅓ cup water
1 tablespoon sesame oil
3 large tomatoes, cored and cut into ½-inch slices
Fresh cilantro or parsley for garnish (optional)
Toasted almonds for garnish (optional)

Heat vinegar, sugar, ginger, and water and stir until sugar dissolves. Stir in oil. Remove from heat and cool. Place tomato slices in plastic container and pour cooled sauce over them. Marinate in refrigerator at least 4 hours. To serve, garnish with cilantro or parsley and toasted almonds, if desired. Makes 4 servings.

Jícama Citrus Salad

1 small jícama (about 1 pound) peeled and cut into ¾-inch cubes
½ cup orange juice
¼ teaspoon salt
2 red apples, cut into cubes
4 tangerines, peeled, broken into sections, with seeds removed
2 tablespoons chopped fresh cilantro
1 teaspoon powdered dried chilies
Whole lettuce leaves

Place jícama in large noncorrosive bowl; pour in orange juice and sprinkle with salt. Toss well, cover and let stand at room temperature 1 hour. About 15 minutes before serving, add apples, tangerines, and cilantro and mix thoroughly. Toss every few minutes until time to serve. Season with chilies and add more salt and cilantro, if desired. Scoop salad into lettuce-lined bowl. Makes 6 to 8 servings.

Fruit Melange

See Champagne Brunch for Twenty-four, p. 238.

Christmas Fruit Salad

From Jennifer Phelps of Carlisle, Iowa

1 egg
1 tablespoon apple cider vinegar
1 tablespoon sugar
1 (12-ounce) can Royal Anne white cherries
1 large bunch seedless green grapes
2 large oranges
1 (15¼-ounce) can unsweetened pineapple chunks
2 cups (or less) large marshmallows
1 cup whipping cream

Beat egg. Stir in vinegar and sugar. Cook in double boiler over simmering water, stirring constantly, until custard thickens. Refrigerate at least 1 hour.

Remove seeds from cherries. Halve cherries and grapes. Peel oranges and divide into sections. Cut each section in half and remove seeds. Drain pineapple. Cut marshmallows into quarters with scissors, dipping them in water between snips. Whip cream and fold into cooled custard. Gently fold in fruits and marshmallows. Cover and refrigerate 24 hours before serving. Makes 8 servings.

Apple Salad

From Jennifer Phelps of Carlisle, Iowa

1 cup unpeeled, crisp tart apples, diced
1 tablespoon lemon juice
2 tablespoons mayonnaise or salad dressing
½ cup whipping cream, whipped
1 cup celery, diced
1 cup Tokay grapes, halved, with seeds removed
½ cup chopped walnuts
Lettuce leaves

Toss apples with lemon juice to prevent discoloration. Gently fold mayonnaise or salad dressing into whipped cream. Fold in apples, celery, grapes, and walnuts. Refrigerate. Serve on lettuce leaves. Makes 6 servings.

Rosy Applesauce Salad

1¾ cups hot water
½ cup cinnamon candies ("red hots")
1 (6-ounce) package raspberry gelatin
2 (16-ounce) cans applesauce

Combine water and candies over medium heat and heat until candies are dissolved. Add gelatin; remove from heat and add applesauce. Refrigerate.

NOTE: This is not a molded salad.

A few years back Iowa was named the Jell-O capital of the world. I wanted to know why, so I talked to all kinds of "experts" and got all kinds of answers. Was it because of the state's large elderly population? Did nursing homes and hospitals have a monopoly on the product? Was it because it's hard to have an Iowa church potluck supper without green Jell-O? Who knows. It was all speculation and lots of fun. *Register* staff artist Tom Weinman captured the whole idea beautifully with a drawing of the Iowa capitol as a molded gelatin salad.

Tomato Soup Salad

From Bette Bast of Urbandale, Iowa

1 (3-ounce) box lemon gelatin
¾ cup boiling water
1 (10¾-ounce) can tomato soup
½ cup stuffed olives, sliced
2 tablespoons lemon juice
2 (3-ounce) packages cream cheese
⅔ cup mayonnaise
1 cup chopped celery
¼ cup chopped onion
¼ cup chopped green bell pepper

Dissolve gelatin in boiling water; add tomato soup. Allow to set partially, then stir in remaining ingredients. Chill for several hours. Makes 4 to 6 servings.

Red-Red Salad

From Sue Luthens of Des Moines, Iowa

1 (6-ounce) package raspberry gelatin
2 cups boiling water
1 (16-ounce) can cran-raspberry sauce
1 (10-ounce) package frozen raspberries, undrained
1 tablespoon lemon juice

Dissolve gelatin in boiling water. With wire whisk, fold in cran-raspberry sauce, raspberries, and lemon juice. Refrigerate. This goes well with fowl. Makes 8 servings.

7-Up Salad

Variations of this have been around for years

2 (3-ounce) packages lime gelatin
1 (3-ounce) package lemon gelatin
3 cups boiling water
2 cups 7-Up
1 (8¼-ounce) can crushed pineapple, drained (reserve juice)
2 cups miniature marshmallows
1 or 2 sliced bananas (optional)

TOPPING
1 beaten egg
½ cup sugar
2 tablespoons cornstarch
1 cup liquid (reserved pineapple juice plus water to equal 1 cup)
2 cups whipped cream

Dissolve gelatins in boiling water. Cool mixture and add 7-Up, drained pineapple, marshmallows, and bananas. Pour into 13 × 9-inch dish. Refrigerate until firm. Blend topping ingredients except whipped cream and cook until thick. Cool. Add whipped cream to cooled topping mixture. Spread over set gelatin mixture. Refrigerate overnight. Makes 12 to 15 servings.

Blueberry Salad

From M. L. Sexauer of Ankeny, Iowa

2 (3-ounce) boxes grape gelatin
2 cups boiling water
1 (20-ounce) can crushed pineapple, drained
1 (21-ounce) can blueberry pie filling
1 cup sour cream

1 (8-ounce) package cream cheese
¼ cup sugar
1 teaspoon vanilla

Dissolve gelatin in boiling water. Allow to partially set, then add pineapple and pie filling. Chill. Thoroughly mix together sour cream, cream cheese, sugar, and vanilla, and pour over gelatin. Makes 8 servings.

Good Salad

From Carolyn Dorrian of Des Moines, Iowa

1 (3-ounce) package vanilla pudding
1 (3-ounce) package tapioca pudding
1 (11-ounce) can mandarin oranges, drained (reserve juice)
1 (8¼-ounce) can chunk pineapple, drained (reserve juice)
Water (enough to make 4 cups when combined with reserved juices)
1 (3-ounce) package orange gelatin

Cook puddings in the juice-water liquid until thick. Add gelatin powder to pudding and stir. When mixture is cool, add mandarin oranges and pineapple chunks and blend. Refrigerate. Makes 8 servings.

Blue Cheese–Yogurt Dressing

¾ cup reduced-fat plain yogurt
⅓ cup blue cheese
Salt and pepper

Put yogurt in small bowl and mash in crumbled blue cheese with fork. Season with salt and pepper to taste. Will keep in refrigerator for up to 5 days. Makes about 1 cup.

Creamy Garlic Dressing

½ cup skim milk
2 tablespoons lemon juice
1 tablespoon olive oil
1½ cups (12 ounces) cottage cheese
¼ cup onion, chopped
2 cloves garlic, minced
½ teaspoon pepper

Put ingredients in blender. Cover and blend until smooth, about 1 minute. Put in covered container and refrigerate at least 2 hours. Makes about 2 cups.

Thousand Island Dressing

See Champagne Brunch for Twenty-four, p. 237.

Healthful Vinaigrette

1½ cups cold water
½ cup rice vinegar
¾ teaspoon salt
¼ teaspoon pepper

Combine ingredients in covered jar and shake well. Makes 2 cups.

Lemon Vinaigrette

2 tablespoons extra-virgin olive oil
2 tablespoons lemon juice
1 tablespoon grated lemon peel
1 garlic clove, minced
½ teaspoon salt

In large bowl, whisk together ingredients. Serve warm or refrigerate to serve later.

Poppy Seed Dressing

6 tablespoons rice vinegar
3 tablespoons fresh lemon juice
⅓ cup honey
1 teaspoon dry mustard
1 teaspoon grated onion
1 teaspoon paprika
¼ teaspoon salt
2 teaspoons poppy seeds
¼ cup sugar (more or less, to taste)
About 1 cup vegetable oil

Whisk together all ingredients except sugar and oil. Add sugar by spoonful and continue whisking, tasting as you go until dressing is sweetened to taste. Whisk in oil by spoonful, stopping when dressing has reached consistency you prefer. Makes about 2 cups.

Cooked Salad Dressing

For apple or any fruit salad

1 cup sugar
1 cup water or fruit juice
2 tablespoons flour
2 tablespoons cider or rice vinegar
1 egg, beaten

Combine sugar and water over medium heat and stir until sugar melts. Blend in flour. Add vinegar and blend. Add small amount of heated mixture to beaten egg, then stir egg into mixture in pan. Cook, stirring constantly, until mixture thickens. Let mixture cool before pouring over apple or other fruit salads. Store in refrigerator. Makes about 1½ cups.

Grains

Autumn Spice Muffins

Full of fall flavor

½ cup canned pumpkin
½ cup milk
1 egg
2 cups baking mix (such as Bisquick)
¼ cup sugar
½ teaspoon ground nutmeg
½ teaspoon ground cinnamon
½ teaspoon ground ginger

Preheat oven to 400 degrees. Grease bottoms only of 12 medium muffin cups or line with paper baking cups. Blend pumpkin, milk, and egg with fork in medium bowl. Stir in remaining ingredients just until moistened. Fill muffin cups about ⅔ full. Bake 15 minutes or until golden brown. Makes 12 muffins.

NO-CHOLESTEROL MUFFINS: Substitute skim milk for whole milk and 2 egg whites or ¼ cup cholesterol-free egg substitute for egg.

Corn Kernel Muffins

Good with soups and salads

2 cups white cornmeal
½ cup flour
3½ teaspoons baking powder
½ teaspoon baking soda
1½ teaspoons salt
1½ cups buttermilk
2 eggs, lightly beaten
2 tablespoons unsalted butter, melted
3 to 4 cups fresh corn kernels, scraped from cobs

Preheat oven to 450 degrees. Grease 24 muffin cups and set aside. Sift together cornmeal, flour, baking powder, baking soda, and salt. Lightly stir in buttermilk, then eggs. Do not overmix. Add butter and corn, stirring just enough to blend. Fill greased or paper-lined muffin cups no more than ⅔ full and bake 25 minutes. Makes 18 to 24 muffins.

Cranberry–Poppy Seed Muffins

Pretty and pretty darn good

1¾ cups reduced-fat baking mix (such as Bisquick)
½ cup sugar
½ cup skim milk
¼ cup nonfat plain yogurt
2 egg whites or ¼ cup cholesterol-free egg product
1 tablespoon poppy seeds
1 teaspoon grated lemon peel
½ cup fresh or frozen (thawed) cranberries

Preheat oven to 400 degrees. Line 12 medium muffin cups with paper baking cups or grease bottoms of muffin cups. Stir together all ingredients except cranberries until moistened. Stir in cranberries. Fill greased or paper-lined muffin cups ⅔ full. Bake 18 to 20 minutes or until golden brown. Immediately remove from pan. Makes 12 muffins.

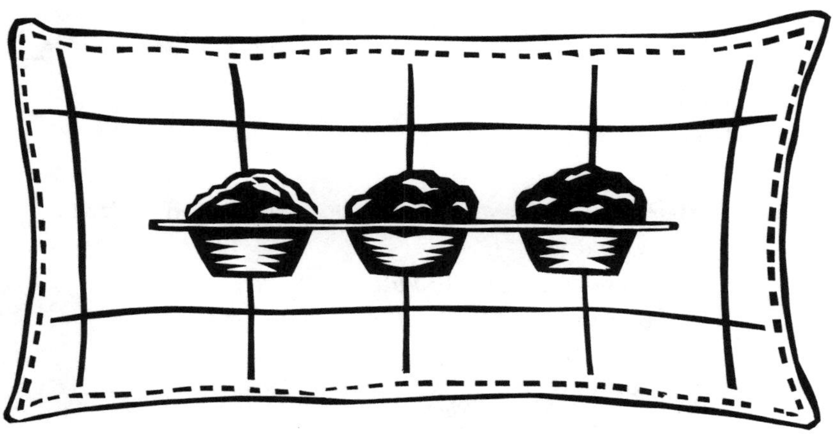

Southwestern Chili Muffins

Just a little zing

1 cup flour
1 cup cornmeal
1 tablespoon baking powder
½ teaspoon salt
1 (8-ounce) can crushed pineapple, drained
1 egg, beaten
1 egg white, slightly beaten
½ cup low-fat milk
¼ cup vegetable oil
¼ cup canned chopped green chilies
1¼ cups Cheddar cheese, diced

Preheat oven to 400 degrees. Combine dry ingredients in large bowl. Combine pineapple, egg, egg white, milk, oil, and chilies. Stir into dry mixture just until moistened. Stir in cheese. Fill greased or paper-lined muffin cups coated with cooking spray ⅔ full. Bake 18 to 20 minutes. Makes 10 large muffins.

Spinach-Cheese Muffins

Unusual and versatile

1½ cups unbleached flour
¾ cup cornmeal
3 teaspoons baking powder
½ teaspoon baking soda
½ teaspoon salt
1 (10-ounce) package frozen chopped spinach, thawed and squeezed dry
1 cup Cheddar cheese, shredded
⅔ cup buttermilk
¼ cup vegetable oil
4 eggs, separated
¼ cup sugar

Preheat oven to 375 degrees. Grease 12 muffin cups or coat with cooking spray. Lightly spoon flour into measuring cup; level off. In large bowl, combine flour, cornmeal, baking powder, baking soda, and salt; blend well. In small bowl, separate spinach into small pieces. Add spinach to dry ingredients; mix with fork until evenly distributed. Stir in cheese. In small bowl, combine buttermilk, oil, and egg yolks; blend well. Add to dry ingredients all at once; mix well. (Batter will be thick.) In medium bowl, beat egg whites at high speed until soft peaks form. Gradually add sugar, beating until stiff peaks form. Fold beaten egg whites into spinach mixture. Spoon batter into muffin cups (cups will be very full). Bake 17 to 20 minutes or until pick inserted in center comes out clean. Cool 1 minute; remove from pan. Serve warm. Makes 12 to 15 muffins.

NOTE: Self-rising flour may be used; if so, omit baking powder, baking soda, and salt.

Stuffin' Muffins

See Back-to-Back Brunches for Twelve, p. 256.

Zucchini Muffins

Another way to use zucchini

2 cups sugar
1 cup vegetable oil
½ cup applesauce
5 egg whites, mixed with fork
1 cup rolled oats
1½ cups all-purpose flour
½ cup whole wheat flour
2 teaspoons baking soda
½ teaspoon salt
2 teaspoons cinnamon
1 large zucchini, shredded

Preheat oven to 375 degrees. Combine sugar, oil, applesauce, egg whites, and oats. In separate bowl, combine remaining ingredients except zucchini. Combine sugar-oil mixture with flour mixture. Fold in zucchini. Fill 24 greased or paper-lined muffin cups ⅔ full and bake 25 to 30 minutes, testing for doneness with pick. Makes 24 muffins.

Authentic Southern Corn Bread

From Jennifer Phelps of Carlisle, Iowa

1⅔ cups white cornmeal
⅓ cup flour
1 teaspoon baking soda
¾ teaspoon salt
2 eggs
2 cups buttermilk
4 tablespoons bacon fat

Preheat oven to 450 degrees. Mix cornmeal, flour, baking soda, and salt. Beat eggs and add to buttermilk. Put fat in 10-inch iron skillet; set in oven until smoking hot. Make well in dry ingredients. Add egg-buttermilk mixture all at once and stir well. Add hot bacon fat to batter and beat well. Pour batter into hot skillet, return to oven, and bake 15 to 20 minutes. Makes 8 servings.

Dried Peach Bread

From Joy McFarland of Ellston, Iowa

⅓ cup shortening
1 cup sugar
2 eggs
1 teaspoon vanilla extract
1½ cups flour, sifted
1 teaspoon baking powder
½ teaspoon salt

¼ teaspoon cinnamon
½ cup milk
1 cup chopped dried peaches
¾ cup chopped pecans

Preheat oven to 350 degrees. Cream shortening and sugar; beat in eggs and add vanilla. Sift together dry ingredients and add alternately with milk to shortening-sugar mixture. Fold in peaches and pecans. Turn into greased 9 × 5 × 3-inch loaf pan. Bake 50 minutes. Cool 10 minutes. Makes 1 loaf.

Honey-Lemon Bread

From Joy McFarland of Ellston, Iowa

2 eggs
⅓ cup butter or margarine, melted
¾ cup honey
½ teaspoon lemon extract
¼ teaspoon almond extract
1½ cups flour
1 teaspoon baking powder
¼ teaspoon salt
½ cup milk
¼ cup chopped nuts

GLAZE
2 tablespoons lemon juice
1 tablespoon honey

Preheat oven to 350 degrees. Beat eggs; stir in butter, honey, and extracts. Sift together flour, baking powder, and salt; add alternately with milk to egg mixture. Stir in nuts. Pour into greased and floured 9 × 5 × 3-inch loaf pan. Bake about 1 hour. Combine lemon juice and honey. Drizzle over bread immediately after removing from oven. Cool 10 minutes and remove from pan. Makes 1 loaf.

Irish Blueberry Tea Cakes

TEA CAKES
1 package blueberry muffin mix
1½ teaspoons cornstarch
½ cup flour
1 egg
¼ cup sour cream
½ teaspoon grated lemon peel

GLAZE
1 egg
1 teaspoon water

HONEY BUTTER
½ cup butter, softened
¼ cup honey

TEA CAKES: Preheat oven to 400 degrees. Grease baking sheet. Drain juice from blueberries that come with mix into small saucepan. Add cornstarch. Stir until dissolved. Cook and stir on low heat until mixture comes to boil and thickens. Remove from heat. Stir in blueberries. Set aside.

Combine muffin mix and flour in large bowl. Stir until blended. Add egg, sour cream, and lemon peel. Stir until dry ingredients are moistened. Work mixture with hands until dough forms. Knead 10 times. Press or roll into 8 × 6-inch rectangle on floured surface. Cut dough into 2-inch squares. Place 2 inches apart on baking sheet.

GLAZE: Combine egg and water. Brush over top of each square. Press in center of each square slightly with back of teaspoon measuring spoon. Spoon 1 teaspoon reserved blueberry filling into center of each square. Bake 10 minutes or until lightly browned. Serve warm. Makes 12 cakes.

HONEY BUTTER: Combine ingredients in small bowl. Stir with wooden spoon until thoroughly blended. Serve with tea cakes.

Pizza Loaf

Kids love it

2 cups baking mix (such as Bisquick)
½ cup processed cheese spread
⅔ cup milk
2 tablespoons chopped green onions
1 egg
1 teaspoon Italian seasoning
⅔ cup chopped pepperoni

Preheat oven to 375 degrees. Grease 8½ × 4½-inch loaf pan. Mix all ingredients except pepperoni until moistened. Stir in pepperoni. Spread in pan. Bake 30 to 40 minutes or until golden brown. Cool 5 minutes; remove from pan. Cool 20 minutes. Makes 1 loaf.

Answering the telephone at the *Register*'s food desk is a way to make a lot of new friends. A man named Steve—that's all we know—calls often with questions. It always makes me feel good when I can give him an answer. It's certainly not that I know all that he asks; I just know where to look for the solution to his problem. What would I do without the ISU Answerline at Iowa State University Extension?

Another "foodie" relationship of long standing is with Andrew Miller of Des Moines, who started calling a number of years ago when his wife became ill and couldn't cook anymore. He called me at work and he called me at home. He almost always knew the answer to his own question; he just wanted someone to confirm it. He had fun experimenting and often gave dinner parties to keep in touch with friends.

Recently he and his wife went into a local residential care facility. When I got a call to do a program for the residents, there was no question that he would be there, right in the front row. He doesn't cook too much anymore, but his interest hasn't waned a bit.

Old-Fashioned Biscuits

See Tea Party for Twelve, p. 248.

Popovers

4 egg whites from large eggs
1 heaping teaspoon nonfat dry milk powder
1 cup cold water
1 cup flour
2 tablespoons butter, melted
½ teaspoon ground cinnamon

Preheat oven to 450 degrees. Spray 6 (6-ounce) custard cups with cooking spray. In blender or mixer, blend ingredients until smooth. Fill custard cups half full. Place cups directly on middle rack of oven and bake 20 minutes. Reduce temperature to 350 degrees and continue baking until very brown, about 15 minutes longer. Serve immediately. Makes 6 popovers.

Pumpkin-Apple Gingerbread

Perfect for autumn

GINGERBREAD
3½ cups flour
1 tablespoon baking powder
2½ teaspoons ground ginger
½ teaspoon baking soda
½ teaspoon salt
½ teaspoon pumpkin pie spice
1 cup butter or margarine, softened
1 cup granulated sugar
½ cup packed brown sugar
4 eggs

1¾ cups (16-ounces) canned pumpkin
½ cup molasses
1 large pippin or Granny Smith apple, peeled, cored, and shredded (about 1 cup)
Powdered sugar

HARD SAUCE
1 cup softened butter
4 cups sifted powdered sugar

GINGERBREAD: Preheat oven to 350 degrees. Combine flour, baking powder, ginger, baking soda, salt, and pumpkin pie spice in medium bowl. Cream butter and sugars in large mixing bowl until light and fluffy. Add eggs, two at a time, beating well after each addition. Add pumpkin, molasses, and apple; beat well. Add flour mixture; mix until well blended. Spoon batter into greased and floured 12-cup Bundt pan. Bake 1 hour or until wooden pick comes out clean. Cool on wire rack 15 minutes; remove from pan. Dust with powdered sugar before serving warm with Hard Sauce. Recipe can be made in 2 (8- or 9-inch) round cake pans or a 13 × 9-inch pan; bake 40 to 45 minutes. Makes 1 cake.

HARD SAUCE: Beat ingredients in small bowl until smooth. Serve warm over gingerbread.

Bread Bowl Chili

A fun way to serve chili

1 loaf frozen white bread dough
2 pounds prepared or homemade chili or stew
½ cup shredded cheese of choice
4 teaspoons sliced green onions

Preheat oven to 375 degrees. Thaw bread dough according to package directions. Divide dough into four equal pieces and roll out each piece into a circle. Place 4 oven-proof bowls (2½ inches deep × 5 inches diameter), greased on outside, upside down on cookie sheet. Stretch dough pieces over bowls. Cover and let set 20 minutes. Remove cover and bake 25 to 30 minutes. Lift bread and remove oven-proof bowls; place bread bowls right-side up on cookie sheet. Continue baking 5 to 7 minutes longer or until bread is golden brown on inside. Cool 10 minutes. Heat chili and fill bowls. Top with cheese and onions. Serve immediately. Makes 4 servings.

Pepperoni Bread Twists

Good with salads and casseroles

1 loaf frozen bread dough (white or honey wheat), thawed
2 tablespoons melted butter or margarine, divided
1 teaspoon garlic powder
¾ cup finely chopped pepperoni
½ cup grated mozzarella cheese
½ cup grated Parmesan cheese, divided

Preheat oven to 375 degrees. Roll out dough into 12 × 10-inch rectangle. Brush dough with 1 tablespoon butter. Top with garlic powder. Evenly sprinkle pepperoni and mozzarella over garlic powder. Sprinkle with ¼ cup Parmesan. Fold dough in half so it measures about 5 × 12 inches. Seal edges and pat down dough.

With knife, evenly divide dough into 8 to 12 slices. Gently pull and twist each piece and place 2 inches apart on greased cookie sheet. Brush with remaining 1 tablespoon butter and top with remaining ¼ cup Parmesan. Let rise in warm place until puffy (30 minutes to 1 hour). Bake 12 to 15 minutes or until golden brown. Remove from cookie sheet immediately to cool on wire rack. Makes 8 to 12 bread sticks.

Blue Ribbon Challah

From Karen Engman of Des Moines, Iowa

½ cup dark brown sugar
2 (¼-ounce) packages rapid-rising yeast
1 tablespoon salt
1¾ cups warm water (105 to 115 degrees)
½ cup unsalted butter or margarine, melted
4 extra-large eggs at room temperature, beaten
7 cups (or more) unbleached, sifted flour
1 egg beaten with 2 tablespoons milk or water
Poppy or sesame seeds (optional)

Combine sugar, yeast, salt, and warm water in bowl. Let stand 5 minutes or until mixture looks foamy. Add melted butter and beaten eggs and mix. Add half the flour slowly and mix. All this can be done with an electric mixer. Switching to dough hook attachment, gradually add rest of flour. Turn dough out on floured surface; knead until smooth. Add more flour if dough is too sticky.

Place dough in well-oiled bowl, cover with plastic wrap, and let rise in warm place 40 to 60 minutes, until doubled. Punch down dough and gently knead out air bubbles, then cover and let rest 10 minutes to relax gluten. Divide dough into thirds for 3 small loaves.

Taking portion for 1 loaf, divide into thirds and roll each third into cord the length of loaf pan. Set 3 cords side by side and braid from center to one end, pinching ends together. Braid from center to other end; pinch to seal.

Place in well-oiled loaf pan or on oiled cookie sheet; cover and let rise in warm place 30 minutes or until doubled. Brush with mixture of egg and milk or water. Sprinkle top with poppy or sesame seeds, if desired. Bake in preheated 350-degree oven 35 to 55 minutes, depending on size of loaf. Cover lightly with foil if bread starts to get too brown. Makes 3 loaves.

VARIATIONS

Poppy Seed: Mix together 1 can poppy seed filling, 4 tablespoons honey, and ½ to 1 cup finely chopped walnuts. Before braiding loaf, roll each cord flat and spread with filling, then roll dough back up into cords and seal edges carefully. Braid the three parts and proceed as indicated in basic recipe. (Don't worry if some filling oozes out.)

Raisin: Add 2 cups raisins, plumped, to dough with last half of flour. To plump raisins, soak in boiling water 5 minutes and drain well.

Onion: Finely chop and sauté 2 to 3 onions; add to dough with last half of flour. (Additional flour may be needed.)

Herb: Add 2 to 3 tablespoons fresh chopped dill to dough.

Pesto: Before braiding loaf, roll each cord flat and spread with basil pesto; sprinkle with pine nuts. Roll dough back up into cords and seal edges carefully. Braid the three parts and proceed as indicated in basic recipe.

Cinnamon Rolls

From Marjorie Burkgren of Dayton, Iowa

1 tablespoon active dry yeast
¼ cup warm water
¼ cup sugar
1 teaspoon salt
¾ cup butter or margarine, divided
1 cup hot milk
2 eggs
3½ to 4½ cups Better for Bread flour
½ cup granulated sugar
½ cup brown sugar
1 tablespoon cinnamon
Favorite powdered sugar icing

Preheat oven to 350 degrees. Dissolve yeast in warm water. Mix together sugar, salt, and ½ cup butter and pour hot milk over mixture. Cool to lukewarm. Add to yeast mixture. Add eggs. Beat well, adding flour slowly to make dough easy to work. Place dough in well-greased bowl; cover. Let rise in warm place until doubled. When dough has doubled in size, roll out into rectangle on floured surface. Spread with ¼ cup butter and sprinkle with mixture of granulated sugar, brown sugar, and cinnamon. Roll up as for jelly roll. Cut into rolls of desired size and place in greased pans. Let rise until doubled. Bake 12 to 15 minutes, until golden brown. Frost with powdered sugar icing when cool. Makes 20 to 25 rolls.

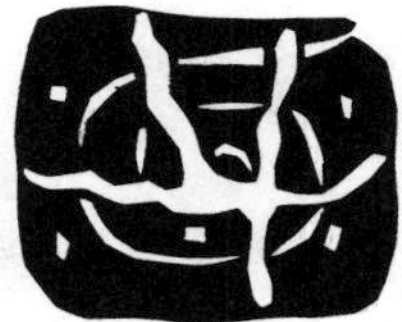

Despite its reputation as a homogeneous "white-bread" state, Iowa has a number of ethnic pockets and, therefore, some wonderful ethnic foods. Decorah and Story City are lefse capitals for Norwegians in Iowa, just as Stanton ("little white city") is for Iowa Swedes. The coffee's always on in Stanton, even on the colorful coffeepot-shaped town water tower. For the Dutch, there are the Pella and Orange City areas. The famous Dutch letter pastries and Dutch spice cookies are musts. The Czech capital is in Cedar Rapids, where you'll want to stop at Sykora's Bakery for poppy seed and fruit-filled kolaches. Among other spots are the Amish and Mennonite areas of Kalona, Bloomfield, and Hazleton, where home bakeries offer wonderful fruit pies and other delicacies on certain days of the week. The German heritage is found all around the state, particularly in spots like Manning and the Amana Colonies. Family-style meals with homemade schnitzel and sauerkraut are specialties at Old World restaurants in the Amanas, one of Iowa's top tourist stops.

Holiday Pull-Apart Loaf

Good for festive brunch

4½ to 5 cups flour, divided
⅔ cup sugar, divided
2 (¼-ounce) packages rapid-rising yeast
2½ teaspoons grated lemon peel
1 teaspoon ground cardamom
¾ teaspoon salt
½ cup butter or margarine, divided
½ cup water
⅓ cup milk
3 eggs
Powdered sugar

In large bowl, combine 2 cups flour, ⅓ cup sugar, undissolved yeast, lemon peel, cardamom, and salt. Cut ¼ cup butter into pieces; heat butter, water, and milk until warm (105 to 115 degrees). Butter does not need to melt. Stir into dry ingredients. Stir in eggs and enough remaining flour to make soft dough. Knead on lightly floured surface until smooth and elastic, about 6 to 8 minutes. Cover; let rest on floured surface 10 minutes.

Divide dough into about 30 equal pieces; roll into balls. Evenly layer 10 balls in bottom of greased 10-inch tube pan with nonremovable bottom. Melt remaining butter. Drizzle about 1½ tablespoons melted butter over dough balls; sprinkle with 2 tablespoons remaining sugar. Repeat layers twice. Cover tightly with plastic wrap; refrigerate 2 to 24 hours.

To bake, preheat oven to 375 degrees. Remove dough from refrigerator, uncover, and let stand 10 minutes. Bake 40 minutes or until done, covering with foil after 30 minutes to prevent excess browning. Let cool in pan on wire rack 10 minutes. Invert onto serving plate. Sift powdered sugar over top and sides of warm loaf. Cool. Makes 1 large coffee cake.

On the Rise White Bread

From Jennifer Phelps of Carlisle, Iowa

5½ to 6½ cups flour, divided
2 (¼-ounce) packages active dry yeast
2 tablespoons sugar
1 tablespoon salt
½ cup softened butter
2½ cups hot water
Vegetable oil

Preheat oven to 400 degrees. Combine 2 cups of flour with undissolved yeast, sugar, and salt in large bowl. Stir to blend. Add butter and water. Beat with electric mixer at medium speed 2 minutes, scraping sides of bowl occasionally. Add 1 cup more flour and beat at high speed 1 minute. Gradually stir in just enough remaining flour with wooden spoon to make soft dough that leaves sides of bowl. Turn onto floured breadboard and knead 5 to 10 minutes or until dough is smooth and elastic. Cover with plastic wrap and clean towel. Let rest 20 minutes. Punch down. Divide dough in half. Shape into 2 loaves and place in greased 8½ × 4½-inch loaf pans. Brush dough lightly with oil. Let rest until dough has doubled, about 1 hour. Bake 30 to 40 minutes or until done. Makes 2 loaves.

Comfort food is part of Iowa. A food page in 1985, for example, told of 1900 farmhouse dinners, cooked over a wood stove at Living History Farms in Urbandale. The headline, "Past Perfect: An Evening in Another Era," was to pique interest in the weekend dinners that were to be served in the historically accurate farmhouse kitchen. Instead, the response caused the farms to serve dinners every night of the week from October through the next spring. A decade later, the dinners are still popular. Standard fare includes beef or chicken, fist-sized dinner rolls, and sing-alongs around a pump organ.

Carbos

Bumble Bee Beans

Pretty to look at, delicious to eat

1 tablespoon olive oil
1 medium onion, chopped
1 clove garlic, minced
3 (15-ounce) cans black beans
1 (10-ounce) package yellow rice mix
Garnishes (optional)

Heat oil in large saucepan or skillet and sauté onion and garlic over medium heat until soft, about 5 minutes. Add 1 can undrained black beans to pan and mash beans with potato masher. Add remaining beans, undrained, and heat through. Meanwhile, cook rice according to package directions. Put rice on plate. Dribble strips of black beans across bright yellow rice. Garnish with fresh cilantro leaves, chopped hard-cooked eggs, sliced green onions, and/or orange slices, if desired. Makes 4 servings.

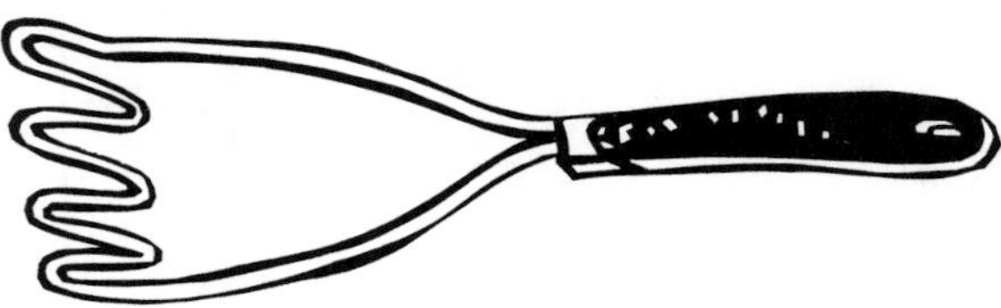

Jean Tallman, food editor of the late *Des Moines Tribune* for twenty-eight years, recalled in a farewell story in 1975 that the stories readers related when they called about a lost recipe were priceless. "My favorite lost recipe stories concern curtains," she wrote. "It seems a kitchen curtain is a favored filing place for a favored recipe. Pin it up there, and it's handy. One reader—filled with chagrin—confessed to washing the curtain with a favorite recipe on it. Another blamed her parakeet for her lost recipe. In a brief soar of freedom, he flew to the curtain and ate ingredients off the recipe pinned there."

Calico Beans

Great for a potluck picnic

1 pound ground beef (optional)
½ pound bacon, cut into small pieces
½ cup onion, chopped
1 clove garlic, minced
1 (16-ounce) can pork and beans
1 (16-ounce) can kidney beans
1 (16-ounce) can lima beans, with half of liquid drained
½ cup ketchup
½ cup brown sugar
1 tablespoon vinegar
1 teaspoon dry mustard

Preheat oven to 350 degrees. Brown beef (if desired), bacon, onion, and garlic; drain. In Dutch oven or large casserole, combine sautéed mixture with remaining ingredients. Bake 30 to 40 minutes. Makes 8 to 12 servings.

Cowboy Beans

2 cups dried pinto beans
5½ cups water
1½ cups chopped onion
2 cloves garlic, chopped
2 bay leaves
¼ pound salt pork, cut into 1-inch cubes
2 cups canned tomatoes
½ cup green bell pepper, finely chopped
2 teaspoons chili powder
2 tablespoons brown sugar
½ teaspoon dry mustard
¼ teaspoon oregano
Salt to taste

Soak beans overnight. Drain. Add 5½ cups water. Add onion, garlic, bay leaves, and salt pork. Cover and bring to boil. Reduce heat and simmer 1 to 1½ hours. Add remaining ingredients except salt. Bring to boil. Reduce heat and simmer 2 hours. Salt to taste. Makes about 8 servings.

Barbecue Beans

From Ruth Jones of Shawnee, Kansas

2 cups dried pinto beans
5 cups water
4 tablespoons bacon drippings
5 tablespoons brown sugar, divided
4 tablespoons butter or margarine
1 large onion, chopped
1 (8-ounce) can tomato sauce
1 tablespoon white vinegar
2½ teaspoons prepared yellow mustard
½ teaspoon prepared horseradish
⅛ teaspoon garlic powder
Salt to taste

Soak beans overnight. Drain. Put beans in 5 cups water with drippings and 2 tablespoons brown sugar. Bring to boil. Reduce heat and simmer several hours or until tender. Meanwhile, in saucepan over medium heat, melt butter; add onion and cook until tender but not browned. Add remaining ingredients and cook on low heat 5 minutes. When beans are tender, add tomato-onion mixture; mix thoroughly and add salt to taste. Pour into 2-quart casserole. Bake about 30 minutes in preheated 375-degree oven. Makes about 8 servings.

Gingersnap Beans

¼ cup onions, finely chopped
1 tablespoon vegetable oil
2 (16-ounce) cans pork and beans in tomato sauce
½ cup gingersnaps (7 cookies), finely crushed
¼ cup ketchup
2 tablespoons light molasses

Preheat oven to 350 degrees. Sauté onions in oil. In oven-proof casserole, combine pork and beans, gingersnaps, ketchup, molasses, and sautéed onion. Bake 30 minutes or until heated through or longer if you prefer drier beans. Makes 6 to 8 servings.

Soulful Black-Eyed Peas

1 pound dried black-eyed peas
1 tablespoon olive oil
1 cup chopped onion
2 cloves garlic, crushed
4 cups water
1 teaspoon salt
1 teaspoon ground thyme
2 bay leaves
¼ teaspoon red pepper flakes

Wash and drain peas. Soak 1 hour or longer in water to cover; drain and set aside. Coat large, heavy saucepan lightly with oil. Add onion and cook over medium heat, stirring often, until onion begins to brown, about 5 minutes. Stir in garlic. Add water, salt, thyme, bay leaves, and pepper flakes. Bring to boil, add drained black-eyed peas, and return to boil. Turn heat to lowest setting, cover, and cook 45 minutes to 1 hour or until peas are tender. Makes 8 servings.

Grandma's Macaroni and Sour Cream

From Jennifer Phelps of Carlisle, Iowa

1 (8-ounce) package elbow macaroni
3 tablespoons butter
1 pint sour cream
Soft bread crumbs
Salt and pepper to taste

Cook macaroni in boiling salted water until tender; drain. Stir 2 tablespoons butter into hot macaroni. When butter melts, add sour cream and transfer to buttered casserole. Top with bread crumbs, dot with remaining 1 tablespoon butter, and season with salt and pepper. Cook under broiler until bread crumbs are lightly brown. Makes 8 servings.

Noodles Romanoff

1 (8-ounce) package egg noodles
1½ cups large-curd cottage cheese
1 clove garlic, minced
½ pint sour cream
4 green onions, chopped
½ cup grated Parmesan cheese
Paprika

Preheat oven to 350 degrees. Cook noodles in boiling salted water until tender; drain. Stir together cottage cheese, garlic, and sour cream. Combine noodles, cottage cheese mixture, and onions in greased casserole. Sprinkle cheese and paprika over top. Bake 25 minutes. Makes 8 to 10 servings.

Pasta with Sugar Snap Peas

A garden-inspired dish

1 pound linguine
Olive oil
1 tablespoon chopped garlic
4 carrots, peeled and cut into thin rounds
½ head broccoli, cut into florets and stems discarded
1 pint ripe cherry tomatoes, halved
½ pound sugar snap peas, trimmed
1 bunch scallions, cut into 1-inch lengths
1 bunch fresh basil leaves, washed and roughly torn
½ cup grated Parmesan cheese

In large pot of boiling salted water, cook pasta until firm but tender. Drain and reserve. Meanwhile, put enough oil in large skillet to coat bottom of pan; sauté garlic, carrots, and broccoli 2 to 3 minutes or until crisp-tender. Add cherry tomatoes and cook 2 minutes. Add sugar snap peas and scallions and cook 1 minute. Toss vegetables, basil, pasta, and cheese together and serve. Makes 4 servings.

Pronto Pasta

Use vegetables on hand

1 cup sour cream
½ cup grated Parmesan cheese
1 tablespoon dry Italian salad dressing mix (half of 0.7-ounce package)
3 tablespoons butter
4 cups fresh broccoli florets, red pepper strips, sliced zucchini, sliced mushrooms, or any vegetable combination
8 ounces uncooked fettuccine

Combine sour cream, cheese, and dressing mix; set aside. Melt butter in large skillet. Sauté vegetables until crisp-tender, about 5 to 7 minutes. Meanwhile, cook noodles according to package directions. Drain; add noodles to skillet with vegetables. Stir in sour cream mixture. Toss gently over low heat until combined and heated through. Serve immediately. Makes 4 servings.

Tradition dies hard. Forever, it seems, Wednesday has been "food day" in the newspaper. The late *Des Moines Tribune* was thick with food ads on that day. Cooks waited for the ads before doing their weekly shopping, which usually was done late in the week. Now consumers shop anytime—seven days a week, twenty-four hours a day—in many Iowa supermarkets. Interestingly, however, in the early 1990s, Hy-Vee Food Stores, a chain based in Chariton, Iowa, tried to move its main advertising to Sundays. Consumers railed and complained. The advertising was moved back to Wednesdays.

Buffet Potatoes

Everyone loves 'em

1 (2-pound) package frozen hash brown potatoes
½ cup butter, melted
1 pint sour cream
1 (10¾-ounce) can condensed chicken soup
½ cup onion, chopped
2 cups shredded Cheddar cheese
½ teaspoon pepper
1½ cups corn flake crumbs
¼ cup melted butter

Preheat oven to 350 degrees. Blend potatoes and ½ cup melted butter. Stir in sour cream, soup, onion, cheese, and pepper. Place in greased 13 × 9-inch pan. Combine crumbs and ¼ cup melted butter; sprinkle on top. Cover with foil. Bake 20 minutes. Uncover and bake 20 minutes more. Makes 10 to 12 servings.

New Potatoes with Parsley

1 pound small new white or red potatoes, scrubbed (unpeeled)
2 tablespoons butter or margarine
3 tablespoons minced fresh parsley
3 tablespoons green onions, green tops only, chopped
Salt and pepper to taste

Cut potatoes in half lengthwise; place in 4-quart saucepan with water to cover. Cover and boil until tender. Drain. Add butter, parsley, and green onions. Toss until butter melts. Continue cooking to wilt vegetables. Season with salt and pepper to taste. Makes 4 to 6 servings.

Garlicky Oven-Fries

From Nancy Catena of San Francisco

¼ cup olive oil
2 cloves garlic, chopped
6 medium russet potatoes, peeled or unpeeled
Pepper
Salt

Preheat oven to 450 degrees. Peel potatoes if you wish and cut each into approximately 8 lengthwise strips. Soak potato strips in ice water for at least 30 minutes. Remove from water and dry thoroughly. Meanwhile, sauté garlic in oil and discard garlic. Pour small amount of flavored oil into bottom of jellyroll pan or cookie sheet. Swirl potato strips in oil to coat on all sides. Spread strips out so they don't touch. Pepper to taste. Bake 45 minutes to 1 hour, until brown and cooked through, turning after 30 minutes. Salt lightly just before serving. Makes 6 servings.

Potatoes with Chives

See Holiday Dinner, p. 266.

Hash-Brown Sweet Potatoes

6 medium sweet potatoes
Butter
2 apples, sliced
½ cup raisins
Ground cinnamon and nutmeg to taste

Peel and shred sweet potatoes. Form into patties and fry in butter (preferably clarified butter) until brown and crispy. Sauté apples and raisins in butter, dust with cinnamon and nutmeg, and serve with sweet potatoes. Makes 10 servings.

Sweet Potato Skillet

See Holiday Dinner, p. 266.

Chop-Chop Fried Rice

From Jennifer Phelps of Carlisle, Iowa

1 cup rice
1½ cups boiling water
¼ cup peanut oil
1 egg, beaten
1 teaspoon salt
¼ teaspoon pepper
¼ cup finely chopped green onions and tops
1½ tablespoons soy sauce

Add rice to boiling water, reduce heat, cover, and cook 25 minutes. Remove from heat and leave covered 15 minutes. Heat oil in skillet to about 350 degrees. Add egg and cook 2 to 3 minutes, breaking into pieces. Add cooked rice, salt, pepper, onions, and soy sauce. Blend well and cook 7 to 8 minutes. Makes 4 servings.

Green Rice

From Ruth Jones of Shawnee, Kansas

RICE
3 cups cooked rice
1 cup chopped parsley
½ cup Cheddar cheese, grated
⅓ cup onion, finely chopped
¼ cup green bell pepper, finely chopped
½ teaspoon garlic powder

SAUCE
1 (14½-ounce) can evaporated milk
3 tablespoons milk
2 eggs, beaten
Scant ½ cup vegetable oil
½ teaspoon seasoned salt
1 teaspoon salt
½ teaspoon pepper
¼ teaspoon M.S.G. (optional)
1 lemon, juice and grated rind
Paprika

Preheat oven to 350 degrees. In mixing bowl, stir together all rice ingredients. In separate bowl, blend together all sauce ingredients except paprika. Pour over rice and mix thoroughly. Put mixture in 2-quart greased casserole; sprinkle paprika on top. Bake 45 minutes. Makes 6 servings.

Rice Ring

See Champagne Brunch for Twenty-four, p. 235.

Easy Risotto

2 tablespoons unsalted butter
2 tablespoons olive oil
½ cup minced yellow onion (about ¼ pound)
1 cup arborio rice
3 cups chicken broth
2 teaspoons salt
Freshly ground black pepper
Freshly ground Parmesan cheese (optional)

Microwave butter and oil in 10-inch deep dish or $11 \times 8\frac{1}{2} \times 2$-inch dish, uncovered, on high 2 minutes. Add onion and stir to coat. Cook, uncovered, on high 4 minutes. Add rice and stir to coat. Cook, uncovered, 4 minutes. (If using small oven, cook onion 7 minutes; add rice and cook 7 minutes.)

Stir in broth. Cook, uncovered, on high 9 minutes. Stir well and cook 9 minutes more. (For small oven, cook 12 minutes; stir and cook 12 minutes more.) Remove from oven. Let stand, uncovered, 5 minutes to let rice absorb remaining liquid, stirring several times. Stir in salt, pepper, and cheese, if desired. Makes 3 first-course servings or 6 side-dish servings.

Spanish Rice

From Jennifer Phelps of Carlisle, Iowa

1 (8-ounce) can tomato sauce
4 cups water
Dash of Tabasco sauce
2 cups long-grain rice
1 tablespoon bacon fat
1 large onion, chopped
1 clove garlic, minced
8 ounces mushrooms, sliced

1 tablespoon olive oil
1 teaspoon dried basil leaves
Dash of Worcestershire sauce
Salt and pepper to taste
1 red or green bell pepper, finely chopped
¼ cup fresh parsley, snipped

Combine tomato sauce, water, and Tabasco in saucepan. Bring to boil. Meanwhile, in large skillet, brown rice in bacon fat. Add rice to tomato mixture and cover. Cook over low heat 25 minutes or until all liquid is absorbed and rice is tender. Sauté onion, garlic, and mushrooms in oil. Season with basil, Worcestershire, and salt and pepper to taste. Add cooked rice, bell pepper, and parsley. Makes 6 servings.

VARIATIONS
New Mexican Rice: Do not use mushrooms. Add 1 (4½-ounce) can mild green chilies, chopped, and 1 teaspoon chili powder to tomato sauce mixture before adding rice. Add ½ cup sliced black olives with bell pepper and garnish with chopped cilantro instead of parsley. Makes about 8 servings.
Hamburger Rice: Brown 1 pound hamburger with onions, garlic, and mushrooms. Makes about 8 servings.

Apple and Walnut Stuffing

From Sandy and Lon Lindenberg of Bondurant, Iowa

1 onion
1 tablespoon butter
1 large sour apple
12 walnuts
½ to 1 pound pork sausage, browned and drained
1¼ cups dry bread crumbs
½ teaspoon powdered herbs, mixed
1 egg, beaten
Salt and pepper to taste
Milk, as needed

Finely chop onion. Sauté in butter until soft and golden brown. Peel, core and chop apple; chop walnuts. Combine onion with remaining ingredients and mix thoroughly. Add enough milk to moisten. Use for stuffing roast duck or goose.

Corn Bread–Mushroom Dressing

A holiday specialty

½ cup butter or margarine
1 medium onion, finely chopped
1 cup finely chopped celery
4 ounces mushrooms, finely chopped
1 (16-ounce) bag corn bread stuffing
1 to 2 cups crumbled dry corn bread
2 (7-ounce) cans chopped green chilies
1 cup coarsely chopped pecans
¼ cup fresh parsley, chopped
½ teaspoon ground thyme
2 teaspoons leaf sage, crumbled
Egg substitute to equal 1 egg or 1 egg
About 1 cup chicken stock

Preheat oven to 325 degrees. Melt butter in skillet over medium heat; add onion, celery, and mushrooms and sauté about 7 minutes. In large mixing bowl, combine sautéed vegetables with stuffing, corn bread, chilies, pecans, parsley, seasonings, and egg substitute. Mix well. Add about 1 cup chicken stock as needed to moisten dressing.

Stuff turkey lightly just before roasting. Dressing in turkey should reach 165 degrees. Put remaining dressing in 13 × 9-inch pan sprayed with cooking spray. Bake 30 minutes or until brown. Makes 12 to 16 servings.

Make-Ahead Corn Bread Dressing

See Holiday Dinner, p. 264.

Wild Rice Dressing

1 (4-ounce) package wild rice
4 slices bacon, cut into 1-inch pieces
1 cup onion, chopped
1 cup celery, chopped
½ pound mushrooms, sliced
½ pound turkey breakfast sausage
2 cups dry bread crumbs
1 teaspoon ground oregano
½ teaspoon ground sage
Salt and pepper to taste (optional)

Preheat oven to 325 degrees. Cook rice according to package instructions. In medium skillet over medium heat, sauté bacon until almost crisp. Add onion, celery and mushrooms; continue cooking until vegetables are tender. Cook sausage. In large bowl, combine bacon mixture, rice, bread crumbs, sausage, oregano, and sage. Season to taste with salt and pepper, if desired. Spoon dressing into lightly greased 2-quart casserole. Bake, covered, 35 to 40 minutes. Makes 6 to 8 servings.

Veggies

Dilly Green Beans

A tasty, low-calorie side dish

1 (10-ounce) package frozen cut green beans
2 tablespoons water
1 green onion, finely chopped
2 teaspoons cornstarch
½ cup water
¼ teaspoon dried dillweed, crushed
Dash of black pepper
1 teaspoon cider vinegar
1 teaspoon instant chicken bouillon granules

Put beans and 2 tablespoons water in 1-quart saucepan and cook until beans are tender. Drain. Cover and set aside. In small bowl, blend remaining ingredients. Microwave on high 1½ to 2 minutes or until clear and thickened. Pour over beans. Toss to coat. Makes 4 servings.

Broccoli-Cheese Bake

From Ruth Jones of Shawnee, Kansas

2 (10-ounce) packages frozen chopped broccoli
1 cup medium white sauce (see recipe, p. 158)
1 cup grated Cheddar cheese
Dash of pepper
½ cup saltine cracker crumbs
1 tablespoon melted butter or margarine

Preheat oven to 350 degrees. Cook broccoli according to package directions. Do not overcook. Drain well. Put in 1-quart casserole. Blend together white sauce, cheese, and pepper. Stir into broccoli. Combine cracker crumbs and butter and sprinkle over top of casserole. Bake 30 minutes or until heated through. Makes about 6 servings.

Broccoli with Orange-Shallot Butter

From Julie Trusler of J.T.'s Cuisine, Newton, Iowa

1 shallot, finely chopped
½ cup butter
½ cup frozen orange juice concentrate, thawed
2 small heads fresh broccoli
Salt to taste

Sauté shallot in butter until transparent but not browned. Add orange juice concentrate and whip into butter until mixture thickens slightly. Set aside. Clean broccoli and peel stems. Drop stem-first in pot of boiling salted water so that stems stand upright. Broccoli heads do not need to be completely covered with water. Cook about 5 minutes or until heads turn bright green and broccoli is crisp-tender. Divide broccoli into individual servings. Drizzle with orange-shallot butter lightly over broccoli. Makes 6 to 8 servings.

Besides new gadgets in the kitchen, Iowa cooks have had to adjust to new produce choices. It's not just corn and beans anymore, thank you very much. Supermarkets and farmers' markets around the state now offer such exotic choices as star fruit, Asian pears, cherimoyas, tomatillos, dried tomatoes, jicama, tofu, and portobello mushrooms.

Cheesed Carrots

From Ruth Jones of Shawnee, Kansas

4 cups carrots, sliced
¼ cup onion, finely minced
½ cup celery, finely chopped
3 tablespoons butter or margarine, divided
⅓ pound good melting cheese (such as Cheddar or Velveeta)
½ cup bread or cracker crumbs

Preheat oven to 350 degrees. Cook together carrots, onion, and celery in water until carrots are fairly tender but not soft. Drain. Meanwhile, melt cheese and 2 tablespoons butter over low heat or in microwave. Pour cheese over vegetables. Put mixture in casserole and bake about 20 minutes or until casserole is heated through. Mix bread crumbs with remaining 1 tablespoon melted butter. During last 10 minutes, sprinkle bread crumbs on top of casserole and continue cooking. Makes 6 servings.

Corn Custard

From La Corsette Restaurant, Newton, Iowa

1 cup fresh corn kernels, scraped from cob
2¾ cups milk, divided
1 teaspoon salt
1 cup yellow cornmeal
½ cup butter, cut into 1-inch pieces
3 eggs, separated, at room temperature
2 teaspoons sugar
¼ teaspoon freshly ground nutmeg
4 to 5 drops hot red pepper sauce

Preheat oven to 400 degrees. Generously butter 2-quart soufflé dish. Chop corn kernels coarsely in food processor, using on-off pulses. In medium saucepan, bring corn, 2 cups milk, and salt to boil over medium heat. Slowly stir in cornmeal. Return mixture to boiling and stir until very thick, about 1 minute. Remove from heat. Immediately beat in butter; stir in remaining ¾ cup milk. Blend in egg yolks one at a time. Add sugar, nutmeg, and hot pepper sauce.

Beat egg whites until stiff but not dry. Fold a fourth of whites into cornmeal mixture, then fold in remaining whites, blending gently but thoroughly. Pour into mold and bake 10 minutes. Reduce oven to 375 degrees; continue baking until custard puffs slightly and is brown on top but center is still soft, about 55 minutes. Serve hot. Makes 8 servings.

NOTE: May also be served in individual baking dishes. If using small ramekins, bake at 400 degrees for 5 minutes, then reduce to 375 degrees for 18 minutes.

Grilled Corn on the Cob

1 tablespoon lemon juice
1 tablespoon soy sauce
4 tablespoons olive oil
1 garlic clove, crushed
Pepper
6 ears of corn, husks removed

Combine lemon juice, soy sauce, oil, garlic, and pepper. Pour over corn in bowl. Refrigerate, covered, overnight.

Wrap each ear of corn in foil, twisting foil ends to seal tightly. Cook directly on coals 15 to 20 minutes or on grill 30 to 40 minutes, turning several times. Makes 6 servings.

Hominy Casserole

With thanks to James Beard

2 (15¼-ounce) cans whole kernel corn, drained
2 (14½-ounce) cans white hominy, rinsed and drained
¾ pound Monterey Jack cheese, shredded

1 cup sour cream
1 (4½-ounce) can chopped green chilies
Pepper to taste
Butter

Preheat oven to 350 degrees. Mix together corn, hominy, cheese, sour cream and chilies and put in oven-proof casserole sprayed lightly with cooking spray. Add several grinds of black pepper to taste. Dot top with butter. Bake 45 minutes to 1 hour—long enough to melt cheese and heat through. This can be made a couple of days ahead and kept in refrigerator to let flavors meld.

Snap Peas with Pearl Onions

See Holiday Dinner, p. 268.

Eggplant Bake

1 large eggplant, washed but left whole
2 medium onions, finely chopped
1 green bell pepper, finely chopped
3 cloves garlic, minced
Olive oil
1 (6-ounce) can tomato paste
Dry white wine

Preheat oven to 400 degrees. Pierce eggplant several times with long-tined fork. Put in small pan and bake 45 minutes or until soft. Remove and reduce oven temperature to 350 degrees. Meanwhile, sauté onions, green pepper, and garlic in small amount oil. Peel eggplant and mash meat. Add to sauté mix. Thin tomato paste with enough white wine for pouring consistency. Add to sauté mix. Put in greased 1-quart casserole and bake 30 minutes or until heated through. Or heat mixture gently over medium heat and use to fill pita pockets. Makes 6 servings.

Snow Peas and Sautéed Apples

Delightfully different

1 tablespoon minced fresh ginger
1 tablespoon mild, light-flavored olive oil
3 cups peeled, cored, thinly sliced apples
¼ pound fresh trimmed snow peas
2 teaspoons sesame oil (optional)

Sauté ginger in olive oil over high heat. Add apples and snow peas. Stir-fry 5 minutes. Sprinkle with sesame oil before serving, if desired. Makes 4 servings.

Spinach Squares

See Champagne Brunch for Twenty-four, p. 235.

Chili Tomatoes

A blend of tasty Mexican flavors

6 medium tomatoes
2 cups (8 ounces) shredded sharp Cheddar cheese, divided
1 (4½-ounce) can chopped mild green chilies, drained
¼ teaspoon ground oregano
¼ teaspoon minced garlic
Sour cream
Chopped green onions, for garnish

Preheat oven to 325 degrees. Cut ½-inch slice from top of each tomato; scoop out pulp and seeds, leaving ¼-inch-thick shell. (Reserve pulp for another use, such as sauce.) Invert tomatoes on paper towel–lined plate and let drain 20 minutes. In large bowl, combine 1½ cups cheese, chilies, oregano, and garlic. Spoon mixture into tomato shells. Arrange tomatoes in greased, shallow baking dish and bake 20 minutes or until heated through. To serve, top with sour cream, remaining ½ cup cheese, and onions. Makes 6 servings.

Puffed-Up Turnips

From Jennifer Phelps of Carlisle, Iowa

4 medium turnips
2 tablespoons butter
2 eggs, beaten
¾ cup dry bread crumbs
1 tablespoon onion, finely chopped
1 tablespoon fresh parsley, snipped
1 tablespoon sugar
1 teaspoon salt
1 teaspoon lemon juice

Preheat oven to 375 degrees. Peel and cube turnips. Cook in small amount boiling salted water until tender, about 20 minutes. Drain. Add butter and mash. Combine remaining ingredients and add to turnips. Bake in buttered casserole 25 to 30 minutes. Makes 4 servings.

Calico Squash

A colorful autumn dish

2 medium butternut squashes
½ pound ground turkey
1 cup chopped onion
1 cup frozen whole kernel corn, thawed
½ cup shredded carrots
½ teaspoon ground cumin
¾ cup vegetable juice
1 (4½-ounce) can chopped green chilies, undrained
⅛ teaspoon pepper
¾ cup instant rice, uncooked
¾ cup Cheddar cheese, shredded

Cut squashes in half lengthwise; spoon out seeds. In 5-quart Dutch oven, in 1 inch of boiling water, place 2 squash halves cut-side down. Reduce heat to low. Cover; simmer 10 minutes or until squash is tender. Remove to platter. Keep warm. Repeat with remaining squash halves.

Meanwhile, in 3-quart saucepan over medium-high heat, cook turkey with onion, corn, carrots, and cumin until turkey is browned and onion is tender, stirring to separate meat. Stir in juice, chilies, and pepper. Heat to boiling. Stir in rice. Remove from heat. Cover; let stand 5 minutes. Stir in cheese. Divide turkey mixture evenly among warm squash halves. If necessary, scoop out some cooked flesh from narrow end of squash. Makes 4 servings.

Fiesta Zucchini Squares

1 cup sliced carrots
1 cup chopped celery
4 eggs or 4 egg whites
4 cups sliced zucchini
½ cup chopped onion
½ cup Cheddar cheese, grated
2 ounces canned chopped green chilies
½ cup vegetable oil
½ teaspoon ground oregano
1 cup baking mix (such as Bisquick)

Preheat oven to 350 degrees. Cook carrots and celery in microwave on high 5 minutes or over high heat in pan. Set aside. Beat eggs slightly in large mixing bowl. Add remaining ingredients, then combine with carrots and celery. Pour into oiled 13 × 9-inch baking dish. Bake 40 minutes or until pick comes out clean. Cut into squares to serve. Makes 12 servings.

The *Register*'s food pages reflect the seasons. There are Halloween treats, myriad Thanksgiving stuffings, Christmas cookies, Easter breads, and Rosh Hashanah honey cakes, along with tips for using spring's first rhubarb, late summer's zucchini, and autumn's green tomatoes.

Polka-dot Zucchini Fritters

2 medium-size zucchini, grated
1 teaspoon salt
1 carrot, grated
½ cup red and/or green bell pepper, finely minced
2 tablespoons minced onion
2 tablespoons minced parsley
1 egg, beaten
½ cup flour
Dash of freshly ground black pepper
Vegetable oil, for frying

Combine zucchini and salt in colander; let drain about 15 minutes, squeezing out excess liquid with back of spoon. Combine drained zucchini with carrot, green and/or red pepper, onion, parsley, egg, flour, and pepper. Drop by tablespoons into ½-inch of hot oil in skillet. Fry until brown on both sides. Drain on paper towel. Serve immediately. Makes 4 servings.

Sautéed Zucchini

From Ruth Jones of Shawnee, Kansas

Zucchini
Olive oil for sautéing
Green onions
Garlic cloves, finely chopped, to taste
Ground oregano or basil to taste
Salt and pepper to taste
Parmesan cheese, grated

Cut zucchini into diagonal slices, circles, or cubes. Sauté in small amount of oil with onions, garlic, and oregano. Cook 5 minutes or until barely tender, turning several times with wide spatula. Serve hot, sprinkled with cheese.

Zucchini Bake

3 medium zucchini, grated
1¼ cups seasoned croutons
½ cup sautéed fresh mushrooms
½ cup onion, chopped
2 slices bacon, cooked crisp and crumbled
½ cup grated Swiss cheese
¼ cup melted butter or margarine
1 egg, beaten
½ teaspoon garlic salt
¼ teaspoon pepper

Preheat oven to 350 degrees. Combine ingredients. Place in greased 1½- to 2-quart casserole and bake 40 minutes. Makes 6 to 8 servings.

Zucchini Cheese Puff

4 small zucchini, sliced ¼ inch thick
¼ cup sour cream
½ teaspoon seasoned salt
⅛ teaspoon pepper
1 egg
2 tablespoons margarine
Dash of garlic salt
½ cup Parmesan or Romano cheese, grated

Preheat oven to 400 degrees. Boil zucchini in small amount of water until just tender. Drain well and place in shallow 1-quart baking dish. With fork, beat together next six ingredients and ¼ cup cheese. Pour over zucchini and sprinkle with remaining ¼ cup cheese. Bake 15 minutes or until set. Makes 4 servings.

Composed Vegetables

See Elegant Dinner for Eight, p. 245.

Potluck Vegetable Casserole

An "open and dump" standby

1 (15-ounce) can whole kernel corn
1 (10-ounce) package frozen cauliflower, cooked
1 (10-ounce) package frozen cut broccoli, cooked
1 (4-ounce) can sliced mushrooms
1 (15-ounce) can cream-style corn
2 cups Swiss cheese, shredded
1 (10¾-ounce) can condensed cream of celery soup
1½ cups soft bread crumbs
2 tablespoons butter or margarine

Preheat oven to 375 degrees. Drain whole kernel corn, cauliflower, broccoli, and mushrooms. Cut up large pieces of cauliflower. Combine cream-style corn, cheese, and soup. Fold in drained vegetables. Turn into 12 × 7½ × 2-inch baking dish. Melt butter; toss with crumbs. Sprinkle on top of vegetables. Bake, uncovered, 30 to 35 minutes or until hot. Makes 12 to 15 servings.

Ratatouille

⅓ cup olive oil
2 cloves garlic, minced
1 medium onion, chopped
1¼ pounds eggplant, peeled and diced
1 pound zucchini, diced
1 green bell pepper, diced
1 red bell pepper, diced
8 ounces fresh mushrooms, sliced
6 ounces tomato paste
⅓ cup water
2 teaspoons sugar
3 tablespoons red wine vinegar
1½ teaspoons salt
1½ teaspoons freshly ground black pepper
2½ teaspoons dried basil
2½ teaspoons dried oregano

In oil over medium heat, sauté garlic, onion, eggplant, zucchini, and peppers 4 to 5 minutes. Add mushrooms. Cook 2 to 3 minutes. Add remaining ingredients. Cover and simmer 20 minutes. Chill in refrigerator. For best flavor, prepare 1 day ahead. Can be served at any temperature. Makes 8 servings.

Grilled Veggies

Cut desired vegetables into 1-inch pieces. Thread on oiled skewers and brush with Italian dressing. Grill over medium flames until crisp-tender.

Purely Protein

Barbecued Brisket

From Ruth Jones of Shawnee, Kansas
Delicious and oh-so-easy

5- to 6-pound brisket
2 tablespoons liquid smoke
1 teaspoon celery salt
1 teaspoon onion salt
1 teaspoon pepper
2 tablespoons Worcestershire sauce
1½ cups barbecue sauce (see recipe, p. 158)

Place large piece of foil in roasting pan, shiny side up (or use roasting pan with tight-fitting lid). Put brisket on foil. Pour liquid smoke over meat and sprinkle with remaining ingredients except barbecue sauce. Wrap foil tightly around meat and store in refrigerator 10 to 12 hours. Transfer from refrigerator to preheated 300-degree oven. Bake 4 to 5 hours. Uncover and pour off fat, leaving at least 1 cup of pan liquid. Pour barbecue sauce over meat. Re-cover and bake 1 hour. Good either hot or cold. Makes 6 to 8 servings.

NOTE: When serving, cut thin slices in rotation around sides of brisket.

George's Swiss Steak

From the late George Goetz of Davenport, Iowa

1 cup red wine
M.S.G. (optional)
1 clove garlic, minced
2½ to 3 pounds good beef chuck or round steak, cut 1½ to 2 inches thick
1 medium onion, chopped
2 teaspoons butter or margarine
Flour
Pepper
2 tablespoons peanut oil

1 (10¾-ounce) can beef consommé
½ cup beer
¼ teaspoon powdered marjoram
¼ cup fresh parsley, finely chopped
Port or sherry (optional)

Combine red wine, sprinkle of M.S.G., if desired, and garlic in nonreactive bowl. Add meat and marinate in refrigerator 2 hours to overnight. Sauté onion in butter and set aside. Remove meat from refrigerator and reserve marinade. With a sharp knife make ½-inch deep slashes ¾-inch apart on both sides of meat, forming diamond pattern. Flour and pepper meat. Heat oil in skillet and sear each side of meat. Add consommé, reserved marinade, onion, beer, and marjoram. Simmer, covered, turning every 15 minutes. Meat is done when it falls away from the bone or is easily pierced by a fork. About 15 minutes before serving, add parsley. Serve with pan juices. Add 1 tablespoon port or sherry to pan juices, if desired. Makes 6 servings.

Italian Beef

From Sandy Huisman of West Des Moines, Iowa

4 pounds rump roast (trim off fat)
1 (1¼-ounce) package onion soup mix
1 teaspoon ground oregano
1 teaspoon anise seed
½ teaspoon garlic powder
2 (10¾-ounce) cans beef consommé
1 green bell pepper, thinly sliced

Place roast in 4-quart casserole. Combine soup mix, oregano, anise seed, and garlic powder. Sprinkle half seasoning mixture over roast. Add consommé. Arrange green pepper slices over roast. Cook in microwave, covered, on high 10 to 12 minutes or until liquid boils. Simmer, covered, on half power, 30 minutes. Turn roast over. Sprinkle with remaining seasoning mixture. Simmer, covered, on half power, 30 to 40 minutes or until tender. Slice thinly into broth. Serve on Italian bread. Makes 12 to 16 servings.

Italian Meat Pie

From Barbara Kiefer of Des Moines, Iowa

MEAT SHELL
2 pounds ground beef
¾ cup quick or old-fashioned rolled oats
½ cup tomato juice
1 egg, beaten
1½ teaspoons salt (or less)
1 teaspoon oregano
½ teaspoon basil
¼ teaspoon pepper

TOPPING
3 tomatoes, cut in wedges
2 (10-ounce) packages frozen chopped spinach, cooked and drained
3 tablespoons grated Parmesan cheese
6 ounces sliced mozzarella cheese

Preheat oven to 350 degrees. Combine ingredients for meat shell. Firmly pack mixture into bottom and halfway up sides of ungreased 13 × 9-inch baking pan. Bake 20 minutes. Drain off fat. Arrange tomatoes in 3 lengthwise rows, alternating with 2 lengthwise rows of spinach on top of meat shell. Sprinkle Parmesan on top of tomatoes. Cut mozzarella slices in strips and arrange in crosswise rows over top of tomatoes and spinach. Bake an additional 20 minutes. Makes 8 servings.

NOTE: This freezes well.

Easy Steak au Poivre

From Jennifer Phelps of Carlisle, Iowa

⅓ cup dry white wine
⅓ cup condensed beef broth
⅓ cup cognac

1 (2 to 3 pounds) sirloin steak, cut 1½ inches thick
2 tablespoons black peppercorns
2 tablespoons butter
2 tablespoons olive oil
Salt to taste

Combine wine, broth, and cognac in shallow glass pan large enough to hold steak. Add meat and marinate in refrigerator overnight, turning occasionally. Drain steak on serving day, reserving marinade. Crack peppercorns coarsely with mortar and pestle or place in small plastic bag and crack with rolling pin. Pound peppercorns into both sides of steak with heel of hand. Heat butter and oil in large skillet over high heat. Add steak and brown 10 minutes on each side. (Steak will be medium-rare; cook longer for medium or well-done steak.) Remove to heated platter. Sprinkle with salt. Add reserved marinade to skillet juices and bring to boil. Serve pan juices over slices of steak. Makes 4 servings.

I get questions on lots of matters. Last summer a woman called just after she arrived from Florida at the Des Moines airport. She wanted to know where to get "the best steak in Des Moines." She said she had come through a serious illness and had lived on soft food for a year. When she recovered, her husband told her he'd take her anywhere to get a good steak. They picked Iowa and literally flew up for the day. Between lunch and dinner, they were renting a car to tour the covered bridges of Madison County around Winterset. After a couple suggestions, she said they likely would have steak for lunch and dinner.

Yet another young woman called a few years back. Her husband had been in the military and had missed Christmas the year before. Someone had given her a sack of chestnuts. She wanted to re-create a special holiday celebration for him, complete with "chestnuts roasting on an open fire." After some sleuthing, I was able to tell her how.

Rosemarie's Chicken-Fried Steak

From Rosemarie's Restaurant, Dallas, Texas

MEAT
4 pieces round steak, each about 6 ounces
2 cups flour
Salt and pepper to taste
2 cups milk
Vegetable shortening, for frying

CREAM GRAVY
3 cups milk
Pan drippings
2 to 3 tablespoons flour
Salt and pepper

MEAT: Place round steak on cutting board and trim; discard bone and excess fat. With meat mallet, pound each piece on both sides, going over meat twice in opposite directions. Set aside.

Combine flour with salt and pepper to taste. Place milk in separate bowl. Place 10-inch cast-iron skillet (others may be used, but cast-iron will give the best results) over medium heat and add shortening to start heating. Dip steaks in milk, then dredge both sides in seasoned flour, patting to work in flour and seasonings. Test temperature of shortening by sprinkling a few drops of milk into it; milk should sizzle. Add steaks, taking care not to crowd, and cook until golden brown on both sides and fully cooked, 2 to 3 minutes on each side. Serve with cream gravy. Makes 4 servings.

CREAM GRAVY: In heavy 2-quart saucepan, heat milk to scalding; do not boil. Drain excess grease from chicken-fried steak skillet, leaving 4 to 5 tablespoons of pan drippings. Heat drippings over medium heat and stir in flour, 1 tablespoon at a time. Cook, stirring, until flour is brown, hot, and bubbling, then add flour mixture to scalded milk, stirring constantly until thick and creamy. Season to taste. Makes 4 servings.

Spiced Beef or Chicken

From Eliot Nusbaum of Carlisle, Iowa

4 tablespoons soy sauce
2 tablespoons honey
¼ teaspoon salt
¼ teaspoon ground ginger
½ teaspoon crushed red pepper
1 pound steak or chicken, cubed
2 tablespoons peanut oil
3 green onions, whites and green tops, thinly sliced
1 clove garlic, finely minced

Mix soy sauce, honey, salt, ginger, and pepper in bowl and add cubed beef or chicken. Let sit 15 minutes or so. (Be careful—the longer it sits, the hotter it gets.) Heat oil in wok or frying pan and add meat, scallions, and garlic. When meat is browned, add soy-honey marinade and bring to boil. Remove from heat and serve over hot rice. Makes about 4 servings.

NOTE: If you double this recipe, do not double the red pepper; just add a few more flakes.

Company Meatloaf

1 tablespoon vegetable oil
1 medium onion, finely chopped
1 stalk celery, finely chopped
½ cup milk
1½ cups dry bread crumbs
1½ pounds lean ground beef
½ pound ground veal
½ pound ground pork
2 eggs
2 tablespoons fresh parsley, chopped
1 teaspoon fresh thyme, chopped, or ½ teaspoon ground thyme
1½ teaspoons salt
Freshly ground black pepper

Preheat oven to 350 degrees. Lightly grease 9 × 5-inch loaf pan. Heat oil in skillet and sauté onion and celery until transparent but not browned, about 2 minutes. Set aside. In bowl, pour milk over bread crumbs, stir and let stand until crumbs have absorbed liquid. Add rest of ingredients plus sautéed onion and celery and mix well.

Spoon meat mixture into prepared pan. Do not pack down. Smooth and round off top. Bake 1 to 1½ hours or until internal temperature reaches 160 degrees. Remove from oven and top with favorite barbecue or tomato sauce. Let rest for 5 minutes before slicing. Makes 6 to 8 servings.

Everyday Meatloaf

From Catherine Mann of Sioux City, Iowa

½ cup onion, finely chopped
½ cup celery, finely chopped
1 tablespoon butter or margarine
2 pounds ground beef
1 egg

1 cup milk
½ cup dry bread crumbs
1 teaspoon chili powder

Preheat oven to 350 degrees. Sauté onion and celery together in butter and set aside. Mix ground beef and egg together. Add milk, bread crumbs, onion-celery mixture, and chili powder and blend well. Bake 90 minutes. Makes 6 to 8 servings.

Chicken Gumbo Burgers

1½ pounds ground beef, cooked and drained
1 (10-ounce) can chicken gumbo soup
2 tablespoons ketchup
2 tablespoons prepared yellow mustard
Chopped onion to taste

Blend ingredients together; simmer 15 minutes. Serve on buns. Makes 4 to 6 burgers.

Mexiburgers

1 pound lean ground beef
1 (4-ounce) can chopped green chilies, drained
¼ to ½ teaspoon cayenne pepper
1 onion, sliced thin
4 hamburger buns, split and toasted
4 slices Monterey Jack cheese with jalapeño peppers
Tomato slices

Combine meat, chilies, and cayenne; shape into 8 thin patties. Grill or broil patties and onion slices 3 to 5 minutes on each side or until meat is cooked to desired doneness. Place a patty on each bun. Top with cheese, onion, a second patty, and tomato. Serve with condiments. Makes 4 double-decker sandwiches.

North Country Sloppy Joes

From Richard McCartan of Kenai, Alaska

1½ pounds ground beef
1 cup tomato juice
½ cup ketchup
2 tablespoons Minute Tapioca granules
½ teaspoon chili powder

Mix ingredients, brown until done, and serve. Makes 4 to 6 burgers.

Veal Roll

See Elegant Dinner for Eight, p. 244.

Rack of Domestic Lamb Nichole

From John Economos of Urbandale, Iowa

2 lamb racks (domestic, 8-bone, chine bone removed)

MARINADE
3 cups water
½ cup olive oil
½ cup cabernet sauvignon wine
1 teaspoon crushed thyme leaves
1 teaspoon cracked black pepper
1 teaspoon salt

NICHOLE SAUCE
2 ounces brandy
1 teaspoon cracked black pepper
½ cup mango chutney
1 teaspoon shallots
½ teaspoon minced fresh mint

Marinate lamb several hours or overnight. Sear meat in pan to seal in juices. Roast in preheated 300-degree oven 20 minutes per pound or until meat thermometer registers 135 degrees. Remove from oven and let stand 15 minutes.

NICHOLE SAUCE: Mix sauce ingredients together in pan and heat to boiling. Reduce heat and simmer 5 minutes. Makes 4 servings. Note: Sauce is also good with pork tenderloin.

Sweet Pepper Lamb Chops

3 tablespoons olive oil
4 sweet bell peppers, green, red, or yellow, or any combination, diced
2 pounds onions, chopped
2 large cloves garlic, minced
1 tablespoon fresh rosemary leaves or 1 teaspoon ground rosemary
Black pepper to taste
4 tablespoons plus 2 teaspoons red wine vinegar, divided
4 double-thick rib or loin lamb chops, fat trimmed off

Heat oil in large skillet; sauté peppers, onions, garlic, and rosemary until peppers and onion are very soft, about 10 minutes. Season with black pepper. Add 4 tablespoons vinegar; cover and cook over low heat about 15 minutes. Meanwhile, preheat broiler and put chops in broiler pan. Broil chops about 12 minutes for thin chops, about 15 minutes for double-rib chops, turning once. Sprinkle each chop with ½ teaspoon vinegar and top with pepper-onion mixture. Makes 4 servings.

Buttered Fish Bake

20 (1½ pounds) red new potatoes, cut in half
1 medium green bell pepper, seeded and cut into 1-inch pieces
1 medium red bell pepper, seeded and cut into 1-inch pieces
1 medium red onion, peeled and cut into wedges
Salt and pepper
4 halibut, cod, or other mild white fish fillets, each 4 to 6 ounces
Lemon wedges (optional)

HERB BUTTER
3 tablespoons olive oil
2 tablespoons melted butter
1 tablespoon chopped fresh rosemary or 1 teaspoon dried rosemary
4 garlic cloves, crushed

Preheat oven to 450 degrees. Place vegetables on baking sheet. Season with salt and pepper. Whisk together oil, butter, rosemary, and garlic. Drizzle half the butter mixture over vegetables; toss to coat well. Bake on upper shelf of oven 20 minutes or until vegetables start to brown. Stir with spatula and move to bottom shelf of oven. Meanwhile, season fish steaks with salt and pepper and brush with remaining butter mixture. Put on baking sheet or broiling pan and place on upper shelf of oven. Bake 10 minutes per inch of thickness, measured at thickest part, or until fish just flakes when tested with fork. Remove fillets and vegetables from oven. Serve with lemon wedges, if desired. Makes 4 servings.

Carp Burgers

From Tom Kollings of Des Moines, Iowa

1 pint canned carp (see following recipe)
1 egg, beaten
1 small onion, finely chopped
1 tablespoon A-1 sauce

1 teaspoon lemon juice
24 saltine crackers
¼ cup flour

Remove large bones from carp and mash carp with potato masher. Mix all ingredients, adding crackers and flour last, then flatten into patties. Fry in oil at medium heat until golden brown on both sides. Makes 2 to 4 burgers.

Canned Carp

From Tom Kollings of Des Moines, Iowa

1 cup salt
1 gallon water
Fresh-caught carp

Dissolve salt in water. Cut cleaned fish into pieces short enough to stand upright in pint canning jar with 1-inch headroom. Put fish pieces in brine and soak 1 hour. Remove fish from brine and drain on paper towel for 10 minutes. Pack into sterilized pint jars, skin-side next to glass. Adjust lids. Process 1 hour 40 minutes in pressure cooker with 10 pounds of pressure.

Microwave Salmon Steaks

2 tablespoons white wine vinegar
1 tablespoon olive oil
½ teaspoon dried basil, crushed
⅛ teaspoon pepper
2 salmon steaks, each about 6 ounces, or 1 large steak, split
¼ pound (4 large) thinly sliced mushrooms
¼ cup thinly sliced shallots

Combine vinegar, oil, basil, and pepper in an 8 × 8-inch glass dish. Add salmon and turn to coat both sides. Marinate 15 to 30 minutes, turning once. Drain marinade into 4-cup glass measure. Add mushrooms and shallots and stir to coat well. Place salmon in glass dish. Cover with waxed paper. Microwave on high 4 minutes, turning dish once, and let stand, covered, 3 minutes. Fish is done when it begins to flake easily when tested with fork. Microwave mushroom mixture on high, 2 minutes, stirring once. Transfer salmon to hot plate and spoon mushrooms over top. Makes 2 servings.

Snapper or Tuna Plaki

From John Economos of Urbandale, Iowa

1 green bell pepper, sliced lengthwise
2 stalks celery, chopped in diamond shapes
1 carrot, sliced
2 bunches green onions, chopped
½ cup olive oil
1 (16-ounce) can tomatoes with juice
1 teaspoon tomato paste
3 tablespoons fresh parsley, chopped
3 pounds red snapper or tuna
Salt and pepper to taste

Preheat oven to 350 degrees. In good-sized skillet, sauté vegetables in oil. Add undrained tomatoes, tomato paste, and parsley and bring to boil. Pour over fish in baking dish. Season to taste. Bake 35 minutes. Makes 4 servings.

Szechuan-Style Shrimp

From Jennifer Phelps of Carlisle, Iowa

2 pounds fresh large shrimps, peeled and deveined
⅓ cup ketchup
⅓ cup chili sauce
2 tablespoons rice vinegar
2 tablespoons soy sauce
Few drops of chili oil

2 tablespoons sugar
½ teaspoon salt
¼ teaspoon crushed red pepper
3 tablespoons peanut oil
2 cloves garlic, minced
2 tablespoons fresh ginger, minced
4 scallions, chopped, (include some of green tops)

Rinse and drain shrimp; pat dry with paper towels. In mixing bowl, stir together ketchup, chili sauce, vinegar, soy sauce, chili oil, sugar, salt, and pepper. Heat peanut oil in skillet or wok. Add garlic, ginger, and scallions and stir-fry about 30 seconds. Add shrimp and stir constantly 2 minutes or until shrimp turns pink. Pour in chili-vinegar sauce and heat through. Serve over cooked rice. Makes 4 to 6 servings.

There are elegant spots for dining out in Iowa, and there are local roadhouses, such as the steak houses in Morrison, Voorhies, or near Reinbeck, all in northeast Iowa. There's the Derby Cafe south of Des Moines, where homemade pie is a must.

There's the tearoom trend of recent years, where Iowans can take time "to smell the roses" and enjoy a conversation with a good friend. The Blue Willow in Harcourt, Thymes Remembered in Perry, Hannah Marie's in Spencer, or Bette Dryer's Tearoom in Indianola have devoted fans.

In addition, there are home-based spots where your party is the only one in the house for a given meal. You'll find some of the best atmosphere and best food in the state at these spots. Try the egg coffee and the homegrown entertainment at Hook's Point Farm near Stratford; the beef tenderloin, pork roast, or raspberry cheesecake at J.T.'s Cuisine at Julie Trusler's farm near Newton; the themed dinners at the Blue Belle Inn at St. Ansgar; or the orange rolls or melt-in-your-mouth sugar cookies at Doe Run Inn near Runnells. No, you can't drop in. The secret's out. Make reservations.

Never Enough Sweet-and-Sour Pork

From Jennifer Phelps of Carlisle, Iowa

SAUCE
¼ cup cider vinegar
½ cup unsweetened pineapple juice
½ cup brown sugar, solidly packed
1 tablespoon cornstarch
1 tablespoon water
1 teaspoon salt
1 teaspoon Oriental white seasoning (optional)

BATTER
1 egg
¼ cup flour
½ teaspoon salt
2 tablespoons chicken stock

MEAT
¾ cup peanut oil, divided
½ pound pork tenderloin, cut into ¼-inch strips
1 cup green bell pepper, cut into 1-inch squares
1 cup canned unsweetened pineapple chunks, drained
1 cup very firm red tomatoes, cut into 1½-inch pieces

SAUCE: Combine vinegar, pineapple juice, and brown sugar in small saucepan, blending well. In small container, blend cornstarch and water, stirring until smooth. Add to pineapple juice mixture along with salt and Oriental white seasoning, if desired. Bring mixture to boil, stirring constantly. Reduce heat and simmer 5 minutes. Cool.

BATTER: Combine batter ingredients in small bowl. Beat until smooth. Cover and let stand about 10 minutes.

MEAT: Heat ½ cup peanut oil to about 350 degrees. Dip meat into batter. Add to hot oil one piece at a time. Don't put too many pieces in oil at once. Fry until golden. Drain on paper towels and keep warm. Heat remaining ¼ cup peanut oil to about 350 degrees. Add pepper, pineapple, and cooked pork. Cook together, mixing gently, about 2 or 3 minutes. Add sauce, blend gently, cover, and cook about 5 minutes. Fold in tomatoes and cook about 2 minutes. Serve with fried rice. Makes 4 servings.

Pineapple Pork Roast

1 (20-ounce) can pineapple slices in juice
1 medium onion, chopped
1 teaspoon vegetable oil
Salt and pepper (optional)
1½ pounds boneless center cut pork roast
1 teaspoon leaf thyme, crumbled
½ teaspoon ground nutmeg
3 cups cooked noodles

SAUCE
1 tablespoon ketchup
1 teaspoon prepared yellow mustard
1 teaspoon white vinegar
½ teaspoon cornstarch
¼ teaspoon ground allspice

Preheat oven to 375 degrees. Drain pineapple, reserving juice. In Dutch oven, cook onion in oil until soft. Salt and pepper pork roast, if desired. Brown roast on all sides. Sprinkle with thyme and nutmeg. Pour ⅓ cup of reserved pineapple juice over roast. Cover; bake 45 minutes or until meat thermometer registers 165 degrees. Remove to platter. Arrange pineapple slices around roast. Spoon sauce over. Serve with hot noodles. Makes 6 servings.

SAUCE: Combine remaining pineapple juice with sauce ingredients in Dutch oven. Cook, stirring, until sauce boils and thickens. Add pineapple; heat through.

Jeannie's Pork Roast and Dumplings

From Jennifer Phelps of Carlisle, Iowa

ROAST
1 clove garlic
1 teaspoon salt
1 (1½- to 2-pound) pork tenderloin
½ teaspoon caraway seeds

SAUERKRAUT
1 small onion, diced
1 teaspoon butter
1 (16-ounce) jar sauerkraut
½ teaspoon sugar
¼ teaspoon caraway seeds
1 small apple, cored and diced

DUMPLINGS
2 eggs, beaten
2 cups flour
1 cup cold milk
2 tablespoons melted butter
¼ teaspoon salt
4 slices white bread, cubed

GRAVY
2 tablespoons pan drippings from roast
2 tablespoons flour
2 cups chicken broth
Salt and pepper to taste

ROAST: Preheat oven to 375 degrees. Mash garlic with salt and smear over meat. Place tenderloin, fat-side up, on rack in shallow, lightly oiled roasting pan. Sprinkle with caraway seeds. Roast in oven 1 hour 15 minutes or until meat thermometer registers 170 degrees.

SAUERKRAUT: Sauté onion in butter until translucent. Drain sauerkraut and add to onion, along with sugar, caraway seeds, and apple. Cover and cook over low heat 20 minutes.

DUMPLINGS: Beat eggs. Add flour, milk, butter, and salt gradually, mixing well with wooden spoon. Beat vigorously with spoon 5 minutes. Set aside 30 minutes. Bring large pot of water to full boil. Stir bread cubes into dumpling dough and turn out onto floured waxed paper. Flour hands and shape dough into 2 ovals. Drop into boiling water and cook, covered, 15 minutes. Turn dumplings over and boil 15 minutes longer. Dumplings will rise and cook on top of water.

GRAVY: Remove tenderloin from roasting pan. Drain off grease, reserving 2 tablespoons and browned bits in bottom of pan. With wooden spoon loosen bits of browned meat and drippings. Add flour and stir into grease and browned bits with whisk on top of stove over medium heat until mixture (roux) thickens. Add chicken broth and simmer 5 minutes, stirring constantly. Season to taste with salt and pepper.

Slice dumplings and pork and serve with gravy and sauerkraut. Makes 4 to 6 servings.

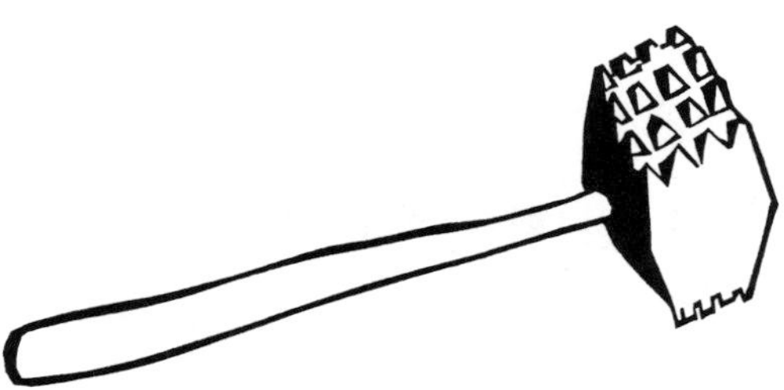

Basil-Stuffed Pork Chops

From Jennifer Phelps of Carlisle, Iowa

4 thick center-cut Iowa pork chops, each about 8 ounces
2 tablespoons shallots, minced
3 tablespoons green bell pepper, finely chopped
1 tablespoon butter
¼ cup Calvados apple brandy or apple cider
10 fresh basil leaves, finely snipped, or 1½ teaspoons dried basil
⅓ cup dry bread crumbs
Salt and pepper to taste
1 tablespoon olive oil
Apple slices, for garnish

Preheat oven to 350 degrees. Cut deep pocket in each chop. Sauté shallots and green pepper in butter until tender. Add Calvados or cider and cook until liquid is reduced by half. Add basil and bread crumbs and season lightly with salt and pepper. Stuff pork chops with bread crumb mixture, closing pockets with toothpicks. (With scissors, snip ends of toothpicks off even with chops so you can brown chops.) Heat oil in skillet and sauté chops until brown on both sides. Stack chops upright in shallow baking pan and bake 1 hour. Remove toothpicks before serving. Garnish with apple slices. Makes 4 generous servings.

Roundup Barbecued Ribs

5 pounds pork spareribs

SAUCE
1 cup water
⅓ cup butter or margarine
2 tablespoons fresh lemon juice
¼ cup dry mustard
¼ cup chili powder
1 tablespoon sugar

1 tablespoon paprika
2 teaspoons salt
1 teaspoon onion powder
1 teaspoon garlic powder
¼ teaspoon cayenne pepper

Preheat oven to 400 degrees. Place spareribs in shallow roasting pan. Cover with foil. Roast 1½ hours. Combine sauce ingredients in medium saucepan; mix well. Bring to boil. Reduce heat; simmer 30 minutes. Brush sauce on ribs. Broil 5 inches from heat 7 to 10 minutes on each side. Serve ribs with additional sauce. Makes 6 servings.

Smithfield Ham and Ham Glaze

See Champagne Brunch for Twenty-four, p. 234.

Asian Pear Chicken or Fish

From Mimi Gormezano of Iowa City, Iowa

4 boned chicken breast halves or 4 fish fillets
2 to 3 tablespoons unsalted butter
Salt and pepper to taste
2 Asian pears, peeled, cored, and sliced ¼ inch thick
4 tablespoons pear brandy or liqueur
½ cup chicken stock (or ½ cup fish stock, with fish fillets)
¼ cup whipping cream
1 teaspoon grenadine or pomegranate syrup
⅓ cup macadamia nuts (pieces or whole), toasted until light brown
Pinch of Chinese Five Spice Powder or coriander (optional)

Remove all fat and tendons from chicken breast. Place between waxed paper and pound thin with mallet. Melt butter in large skillet until it sizzles, then quickly sauté chicken breasts or fish fillets about 1 minute per side. Remove; salt and pepper to taste, and cover with foil to keep warm. Using same skillet, sauté Asian pear slices about 5 to 8 minutes. Remove and set aside with chicken or fish.

Add pear brandy, chicken stock, and cream to skillet. Over high heat reduce liquid until thick enough to coat back of spoon. Reduce heat to low and add grenadine or pomegranate syrup. Slice breasts into diagonal strips (leave fish fillets whole) and add to skillet. Add sautéed Asian pear slices and any juices to skillet. Heat gently until just warm. Add toasted nuts and stir in Chinese Five Spice Powder or coriander, if desired. Serve with rice pilaf, wild rice, or bulgur wheat. Makes 4 servings.

NOTE: Pistachios, pecans, or hazelnuts can be substituted for macadamia nuts.

Chicken Marengo

From Nancy Catena of San Francisco
Delicious over rice and warms up beautifully

2 cups flour
Salt and pepper to taste
3½-pound chicken, cut into pieces (or favorite chicken parts)
2 tablespoons olive oil
1 (8-ounce) can tomato sauce
½ cup dry sherry
½ cup sliced mushrooms
½ cup stuffed green olives, sliced
1 cup chicken broth

Mix flour, salt, and pepper together in shallow bowl. Dredge chicken pieces in seasoned flour, turning each piece to make sure it's coated. In Dutch oven, brown chicken pieces in oil. Add remaining ingredients, stirring into chicken. Cover and cook over low heat 50 to 60 minutes until chicken is tender. Makes 4 servings.

Chicken Supreme

½ cup (4 ounces) ricotta cheese
¼ cup (2 ounces) shredded mozzarella cheese
4 tablespoons (1 ounce) grated Parmesan cheese, divided
1 tablespoon dry bread crumbs

½ tablespoon basil
1 whole chicken breast, split and boned (leave skin intact for stuffing)
¼ cup chopped onion
1 tablespoon cornstarch
½ cup chicken broth
½ cup half-and-half cream
3 tablespoons dry white wine (optional)

Preheat oven to 350 degrees. In small bowl, combine ricotta, mozzarella, 2 tablespoons Parmesan, bread crumbs, and basil. Carefully separate skin from flesh of each chicken breast, leaving one side attached. Spoon half of cheese mixture between skin and flesh of each breast. Secure skin to meat with toothpicks. Place chicken, skin-side up, in shallow baking pan. Bake uncovered until chicken is cooked through and golden brown, about 30 minutes.

Remove chicken from baking pan; remove toothpicks and keep chicken warm. Place onion in baking pan and cook on stove top over medium heat, stirring occasionally, until tender. Combine cornstarch and chicken broth. Stir broth, half-and-half, and wine, if desired, into baking pan; heat until sauce bubbles. Cook over low heat, stirring constantly, until mixture thickens, about 5 minutes. Spoon over chicken; sprinkle with remaining 2 tablespoons Parmesan. Makes 2 servings.

Chicken Sabra

From Michaela Karni of Albuquerque

½ pint Greek olives
¾ cup water
2 cups red wine
1 (6-ounce) can frozen orange juice concentrate
1 or 2 red onions, thinly sliced
2 teaspoons thyme
2 cloves garlic, minced
Salt and pepper to taste
3 cut-up frying chickens

Simmer olives in water briefly, until liquid is reduced to about ½ cup. Add olives and liquid to wine, orange juice concentrate, onions, thyme, and garlic, and salt and pepper to taste. Pour over chicken and marinate 2 hours at room temperature or as long as overnight in refrigerator.

Preheat oven to 350 degrees. Bake uncovered in marinade 1 hour or until done, turning chicken pieces once. Makes 8 servings.

Lemon Chicken

From Germaine Swanson of Germaine's Restaurant, Washington, D.C.

2 to 3 boneless, skinless chicken breasts

MARINADE
1 tablespoon pale dry sherry
½ cup fresh lemon juice
White pepper and salt to taste

BATTER
1 egg white
½ cup flour
½ cup cornstarch
½ cup water
Peanut oil, for deep-frying

SAUCE
2 tablespoons vegetable oil
4 tablespoons ketchup
2 tablespoons soy sauce
1 tablespoon sesame oil
3 tablespoons fresh lemon juice
3 tablespoons sugar
¼ teaspoon chopped fresh ginger
½ teaspoon chopped garlic cloves
½ teaspoon chili or garlic paste (optional)

GARNISHES
1 cup shredded iceberg lettuce
1 teaspoon chopped scallions
1 teaspoon roasted sesame seeds
1 tomato, sliced
½ lemon, sliced

MARINADE: Combine marinade ingredients. Pour over chicken and marinate 30 to 40 minutes.

BATTER: Combine egg white, flour, cornstarch, and water. Coat chicken pieces in batter and deep-fry in peanut oil over medium heat until light golden brown. Drain and cut breasts into bite-sized pieces.

SAUCE: Heat vegetable oil. Combine remaining sauce ingredients, add to hot oil, and stir until just hot.

To serve, put chicken pieces on bed of shredded lettuce. Pour warm sauce over chicken pieces and sprinkle with scallions and sesame seeds. Garnish plates with tomato and lemon slices. Makes 4 to 6 servings.

Precious Chicken

Easy, healthful, and great for a family meal

4 tablespoons soy sauce, divided
2 tablespoons Oriental sesame oil, divided
1 tablespoon cornstarch
2 boneless, skinless chicken breast halves, cut in thin strips
8 ounces uncooked vermicelli
1 tablespoon sugar
2 tablespoons white vinegar
2 tablespoons vegetable oil, divided
1 medium carrot, julienned
¼ pound fresh snow peas, trimmed
½ cup green onions, chopped with some of green tops
1 to 1½ tablespoons fresh ginger, chopped
½ to ¾ teaspoon crushed red pepper

Blend 1 tablespoon soy sauce and 1 tablespoon sesame oil with cornstarch. Stir in chicken. Let stand 10 minutes. Break vermicelli in half and cook according to package directions, omitting salt. Drain and keep warm in large mixing bowl. Dissolve sugar in vinegar and remaining 3 tablespoons soy sauce and 1 tablespoon sesame oil. Set aside. Heat 1 tablespoon vegetable oil in wok or large skillet over high heat. Add chicken and stir-fry 3 minutes; remove chicken from pan. In same pan, add remaining 1 tablespoon vegetable oil. Add carrot and snow peas and stir-fry 1 minute. Add onions and ginger and stir-fry 1 minute. Return chicken to pan and add set-aside vinegar mixture. Pour chicken mixture over vermicelli and toss. Serve immediately. Let diners add red pepper flakes to their individual tastes. Makes 4 small servings.

NOTE: Recipe doubles and triples nicely.

Stir-Fried Chicken and Broccoli

4 boneless, skinless chicken breasts
¼ teaspoon ground ginger
¼ teaspoon pepper
3 tablespoons peanut oil
1 bunch fresh broccoli, sliced thin
1 cup sliced green onions, green tops included
1 cup chicken broth, divided
1 teaspoon salt
½ teaspoon sugar
1 tablespoon cornstarch
¼ cup grated Parmesan cheese

CROUTONS
4 slices whole wheat bread
2 tablespoons butter, melted
1 tablespoon fresh parsley, chopped
½ teaspoon garlic salt

Chop chicken into bite-sized pieces. Sprinkle ginger and pepper over chicken. In large skillet or wok, pour in oil and heat to high temperature. Add chicken and stir-fry 3 minutes or until brown. Push chicken to side and add broccoli and onions. Stir-fry 3 minutes. Mix together ¾ cup chicken broth, salt, and sugar and stir into pan. Reduce heat to medium-high, cover, and cook 2 minutes. Add cornstarch to remaining ¼ cup chicken broth and blend until smooth. Stir into pan and cook 1 minute; remove from heat. Stir in cheese; sprinkle with croutons. Makes 8 servings.

CROUTONS: Preheat oven to 300 degrees. Cut bread into 1-inch cubes. Mix together crouton ingredients. Spread, one layer deep, and toast about 20 minutes or until crisp.

Uptown Chicken and Rice

From Jennifer Phelps of Carlisle, Iowa

1 (2½-pound) broiler-fryer, cut in serving-size pieces
½ cup flour
½ cup chicken fat
2 cups rice
2 medium onions, chopped
2 cloves garlic, minced
2 tablespoons butter
2 teaspoons salt
1 (3-ounce) jar chopped pimientos
1 teaspoon chili powder
½ teaspoon Tabasco sauce

Preheat oven to 350 degrees. In Dutch oven or other large pot, simmer chicken in salted water to cover 1 hour or until three-fourths done. Drain and cool, reserving 5 cups chicken broth. Roll chicken pieces in flour. Melt chicken fat in skillet. Brown chicken pieces in hot fat and transfer to large casserole. Sprinkle rice between pieces of chicken. In large pan, sauté onions and garlic in butter until golden. Add salt, pimientos, chili powder, Tabasco, and reserved chicken broth. Heat to boiling. Pour broth mixture over chicken and rice. Cover and bake until tender, about 1 hour. Makes 4 servings.

Roast Turkey

See Holiday Dinner, p. 262.

Mixed Grill

Hamburger balls
Cheese chunks
Green olives
Dry bread crumbs
Maytag blue cheese
Butter
Cocktail franks
Gherkins
Pitted black olives
Cocktail onions

Form hamburger balls around cheese chunks or green olives. Mix some bread crumbs into ground beef to keep it from crumbling into coals. Baste with Maytag blue cheese melted in butter. Grill cocktail franks on separate bamboo skewers. Serve hamburger balls and franks with pickles, black olives, and cocktail onions.

Grilled Burgers

From Tone's Spices

½ cup chopped onion
2 pounds ground beef
Onion salt
Barbecue spice
Liquid smoke

Blend onion into ground beef and season to taste with onion salt and barbecue spice. Shape into patties and add dash of liquid smoke. Cook over glowing coals.

Grilled Beef

From Tone's Spices

Roast, ribs, chops, or steak
1 tablespoon barbecue spice
1 tablespoon onion salt
Liquid smoke
2½ tablespoons chopped onion
¼ cup vegetable oil
1 cup water
¾ cup ketchup
⅓ cup lemon juice
3 tablespoons sugar
1 tablespoon Worcestershire sauce
1 tablespoon prepared mustard
2 teaspoons salt
¼ teaspoon hot pepper sauce

Use top-grade roasts, ribs, chops, or steaks at least 1 inch thick. Season with barbecue spice and onion salt. Brush with liquid smoke and allow to sit 30 minutes before placing on grill. To make sauce, cook onion in oil until tender but not brown. Add remaining ingredients and simmer 15 minutes. Cook meat slowly over low coals, basting with sauce during last 20 minutes of cooking.

Grilled Salsa Chops

4 boneless pork loin chops, ½-inch thick
¼ cup thick and chunky hot salsa
2 tablespoons orange marmalade
¼ teaspoon seasoned salt

Place chops in plastic bag or nonmetal baking dish. In small bowl, combine remaining ingredients; blend well. Pour marinade mixture over pork, turning to coat. Seal bag or cover dish; marinate about 1 hour, turning chops several times. When ready to barbecue, remove chops, reserving marinade. Place chops on grill 4 to 6 inches above medium-hot coals. Grill about 4 minutes per side, basting with reserved marinade. Serve hot. Makes 4 servings.

Herbed Chops

2 cloves garlic, crushed
1 tablespoon crushed coriander seeds
1 tablespoon coarsely ground black pepper
1 tablespoon brown sugar
3 tablespoons soy sauce
4 boneless pork chops, about 1 inch thick

Combine all ingredients except pork chops. Place chops in shallow dish and pour marinade over; let marinate 30 minutes. Prepare medium-hot coals, banked, in grill bed. Remove pork from marinade and grill chops over indirect heat 12 to 15 minutes, turning once. Or remove from marinade and broil or pan-broil 10 minutes, turning occasionally. Juices should run clear and chops should be tender and juicy. Makes 4 servings.

Grilled Chicken or Turkey

From Tone's Spices

Chicken or turkey
2 tablespoons liquid smoke
¼ pound butter, melted
1 teaspoon barbecue spice
2 tablespoons Worcestershire sauce

Brush meat with liquid smoke and allow to sit at room temperature 30 minutes. Mix remaining ingredients to make basting sauce. Use often while grilling chicken or turkey. Cook meat until golden brown and fork tender.

Grilled Chicken with Mango-Avocado Salsa

10 boned chicken breasts, thighs, or combination (with skin on preferred)
Ground black pepper to taste
Spike or seasoned salt to taste
Garlic salt (optional)
Mango Salsa (see recipe, p. 153)

Line bottom section of broiler pan with foil. Place rack on top. Arrange oven rack to a position about 7 inches from broiler element; preheat broiler.

Trim excess fat and skin from chicken. Season chicken with pepper, seasoned salt, and garlic salt, if desired. Place chicken, skin-side up, on prepared broiler rack. Broil 8 to 10 minutes; turn and broil an additional 4 to 5 minutes until no pink color remains in thickest part of chicken. Chill thoroughly. Serve with Mango Salsa. Makes 6 to 8 servings.

NOTE: For potluck or picnic, garnish chicken with sprigs of fresh Italian parsley or rosemary before packing in ice chest. Pack Mango Salsa separately. Serve cold, spooning salsa over chicken just before serving.

Cranberry Grilled Chicken

From Sandy Huisman of West Des Moines, Iowa

¼ cup cranberry juice concentrate, thawed
2 tablespoons water
2 tablespoons sugar
2 sprigs thyme
⅛ teaspoon salt
⅛ teaspoon pepper
4 boneless, skinless chicken breasts

Combine all ingredients except chicken. Add chicken and marinate overnight in refrigerator. Grill chicken about 3 minutes per side over high heat. Makes 4 servings.

Grilled Turkey Breast

⅔ cup lemon juice
⅔ cup vegetable oil
⅓ cup water
4 teaspoons Dijon-style mustard
1½ teaspoons fresh thyme or ¾ teaspoon dried thyme
2 cloves garlic, finely chopped
1 (1¾- to 2½-pound) boneless turkey breast half

Combine all ingredients except turkey; mix well. In large, shallow dish, pour 1¼ cups marinade over turkey. Cover; marinate in refrigerator 8 hours or overnight, turning occasionally. Chill remaining marinade. Remove meat from marinade. Grill or broil meat over indirect heat 1 to 1½ hours or until meat thermometer inserted in center registers 170 degrees. Baste frequently with reserved marinade. Let stand 10 minutes before slicing. May be served cold. Makes 6 to 8 servings.

Celebrating with food is common in Iowa. Some spots around Dubuque, in northeastern Iowa, have regular Friday night fish frys or fish boils. Lots of graduation parties, wedding receptions, and small-town celebrations also put on hog roasts to mark an occasion. Sometimes the hog is wrapped in burlap, buried, and cooked all night. Other times a large portable cooker goes to the party.

Grilled Fish

From Tone's Spices

1 (1½- to 2-pound) whole fish

SAUCE
¼ cup butter, melted
¼ cup lemon juice
2 tablespoons soy sauce
½ teaspoon onion salt
½ teaspoon barbecue spice
½ teaspoon dried leaf oregano
2 tablespoons water

Use bass, flounder, bluefish, or trout. Place fish on well-oiled sheet of foil and grill 5 inches from coals 12 to 15 minutes per side, turning once. Combine sauce ingredients and heat at edge of grill. Brush fish often with sauce. Makes 3 or 4 servings.

Apricot-Sauced Ribs

4 pounds pork spareribs

SAUCE
1 (8-ounce) can apricot halves, undrained
3 tablespoons ketchup
3 tablespoons brown sugar
2 tablespoons lemon juice
1 tablespoon Dijon-style mustard
1 teaspoon powdered ginger
Dash of salt

Arrange medium-hot coals in covered grill on either side of drip pan. Place ribs over drip pan, cover grill, and cook ribs over indirect heat 1½ hours. Mix sauce ingredients in blender. Brush ribs generously with sauce and continue to cook, about 30 minutes, basting and turning often. Cut ribs into serving-size pieces. Makes 4 servings.

Jerk Ribs

2 tablespoons dried minced onion
1 tablespoon onion powder
4 teaspoons ground thyme
2 teaspoons salt
2 teaspoons ground allspice
½ teaspoon ground nutmeg
½ teaspoon ground cinnamon
1 tablespoon sugar
2 teaspoons black pepper
1 teaspoon cayenne pepper
2 pounds pork back ribs

In small jar with tight-fitting lid, shake together dry ingredients until blended. Rub dry mixture onto all surfaces of ribs. Grill ribs over indirect heat in covered grill, turning occasionally, until ribs are tender, about 1½ hours (or oven-roast ribs on rack in shallow pan at 350 degrees 1½ hours). Cut into 1- or 2-rib portions to serve. Makes 10 servings.

Bambooed Skewer

Beef strips
½ cup soy sauce
¼ cup red wine
1 clove garlic, minced
2 teaspoons ground ginger or 2 tablespoons grated fresh ginger
1 tablespoon sugar
Pineapple chunks
Bamboo shoots
Green bell pepper chunks

Cut thin strips of beef across grain. Marinate in mixture of soy sauce, wine, garlic, ginger, and sugar for several hours. Thread meat, pineapple, bamboo shoots, and pepper chunks on thoroughly soaked bamboo skewers. Grill over medium coals, basting lightly with marinade. Do not overcook; it toughens the meat. Makes 6 servings.

NOTE: Do not salt meat; marinade is already salty.

Chuck's Kabobs

From Tone's Spices

SAUCE
¼ cup onion soup mix
2 tablespoons sugar
½ cup ketchup
¼ cup vinegar
¼ cup salad oil
1 tablespoon prepared yellow mustard
¼ teaspoon barbecue spice
Dash of hot pepper sauce
½ cup water

MEAT
1½ pounds beef chuck
Meat tenderizer
1 red bell pepper
1 green bell pepper

In saucepan, combine sauce ingredients and bring to boil. Reduce heat and simmer 20 minutes, then cool. Pierce meat with fork and cut into 1-inch cubes. Sprinkle with meat tenderizer. Add meat to sauce and toss to coat. Refrigerate overnight. Drain meat but reserve marinade sauce. Thread meat and pieces of red and green peppers on skewers and broil over medium coals 20 to 25 minutes, turning once and brushing with marinade.

Near-Asian Chicken Kabobs

Chicken breast, cubed
Butter
Dry bread crumbs
Parmesan cheese, grated
Pineapple chunks
Mandarin orange slices
Scallions
Green bell pepper chunks
Butter
Soy sauce

Before cooking, roll chicken cubes in butter, then in mix of bread crumbs and cheese. (This prevents chicken from drying out.) Thread chicken cubes, pineapple, mandarin orange slices, scallions, and pepper chunks on thoroughly soaked bamboo skewers. Cook over medium coals, basting with mixture of melted butter and soy sauce.

Chicken Liver Kabobs

Chicken livers
Water chestnuts
Green onions
Bacon
Butter
Sherry
Onion salt

Chicken livers are difficult to skewer but firm up during cooking. They're easier to do under the broiler than on a grill. Use thin, thoroughly soaked bamboo skewers to avoid splitting water chestnuts in two. Snake bacon strips in and out among other ingredients; space food widely so heat can get to bacon. Use butter laced with sherry and onion salt for baste. Grill over medium coals or under broiler. Be careful not to overcook.

Pizza on a Stick

Sausage balls
Mushrooms
Pepperoni slices
Green pepper
Canadian bacon, folded
Crusty roll
Pizza sauce
Mozzarella cheese

Thread first five ingredients on thoroughly soaked bamboo skewers and grill over medium coals until sausage and bacon are cooked through. When done, scoot each skewer's ingredients into crusty roll spread with pizza sauce; sprinkle with cheese and run under broiler until cheese melts.

NOTE: If you're using ground sausage, work in some bread crumbs to help sausage keep its shape.

Seafood Skewer

Zucchini, sliced ½ inch thick
Scallops
Large shrimp wrapped in pimiento strip
Mushroom caps
Butter
Lime juice
Dillweed
Salt and pepper

Precook zucchini slightly so seafood won't overcook. Thread first four ingredients on thoroughly soaked bamboo skewers and grill over medium coals until shrimp turns pink. Baste with melted butter laced with lime juice, dillweed, salt, and pepper.

Skeweiners

For over an open campfire

Commercial refrigerated biscuits
Wieners
Pickles
Cherry tomatoes

Wrap a biscuit in spiral around wiener and thread on thoroughly soaked bamboo skewer. Add pickle and cherry tomato. The dough expands during cooking to make a sort of bun for wiener. One biscuit from tube purchased at supermarket, rolled into string about as thick as pencil, is about right to wrap one wiener. Hold skewers over open fire, turning constantly so dough cooks evenly. When done, dip Skeweiners in ketchup and/or mustard.

Cock-a-Doodle-Kabobs

For those breakfasts around the campfire

Brown 'n' serve sausages
Peach halves
Canadian bacon, folded
Canned crabapples
Melted butter
Fruit juice

Thread first four ingredients on thoroughly soaked bamboo skewers; baste with mixture of butter and fruit juice. Grill over medium coals until sausage is cooked through.

Candied Duck

From Tom Kollings of Des Moines, Iowa

2 large apples
1 cup brown sugar
4 large duck breasts

2 cups flour
1 teaspoon salt
1 teaspoon pepper

Slice apples; place on cookie sheet and sprinkle with brown sugar. Let stand 1 hour or until the juice from apples turns brown sugar to syrup. Fillet breasts; slice meat into strips. Roll in flour with salt and pepper mixed in. Fry as you would chicken until almost done. Pour apples and brown sugar mixture into fry pan with meat. Cover pan; simmer 15 to 20 minutes. Makes 3 to 4 servings.

Pheasant Stifatho

From John Economos of Urbandale, Iowa

2 pheasants (about 4 pounds), cut in serving-size pieces
1 medium onion, chopped fine
Butter, for browning
Salt and pepper to taste
½ cup olive oil
1 (16-ounce) can tomatoes, undrained
2 tablespoons tomato paste
5 garlic cloves, chopped
¼ cup white wine vinegar
¼ cup chopped parsley
3 tablespoons whole pickling spices (tie in cheesecloth or place in a tea infuser)
3 pounds whole baby onions, peeled
1 bay leaf
½ teaspoon ground oregano

Brown pheasant pieces with chopped onion in butter in large Dutch oven. Season with salt and pepper. Add remaining ingredients. Cover and bring to boil. Reduce heat; cook slowly 1½ hours until meat is tender. Rabbit can be substituted for pheasant. Makes 4 servings.

Sandy's Pheasant

From Sandy and Lon Lindenberg of Bondurant, Iowa

1 pheasant, cleaned and skinned
Lawry's seasoned salt
Pinch of garlic powder
1 cup flour
2 tablespoons lard
½ cup water
1 (6½-ounce) box Stove Top dressing
Small can of mushrooms

Cut legs and wings off pheasant breast. Mix Lawry's seasoned salt and garlic powder in flour. Roll pheasant legs, wings, and breast in mixture. In skillet, heat lard on high and quickly brown bird pieces on all sides. Turn heat to low, add ½ cup of water, put lid on skillet, and steam 35 to 40 minutes. Add Stove Top dressing, mushrooms, and enough water to slightly moisten 15 minutes before pheasant is done. Makes 4 servings.

John Economos of Urbandale dished up coneys—hot dogs covered with chili—for forty years. But when he retired, he went upscale and cooked gourmet dishes with pheasant and lamb. "My wife held the house together and raised our three sons while I worked," he says. "Now it's her time to play and rest. I love to cook. My daughters-in-law love for me to cook for their parties. Sometimes I've actually left dishes of food inside the back door as a party was starting near the front door."

Easy Dove

From Tom Kollings of Des Moines, Iowa

12 dove breasts
⅓ to ½ cup water
1 package chicken gravy mix
1 teaspoon salt
1 teaspoon pepper
1 to 2 tablespoons margarine

Preheat oven to 350 degrees. Place dove breasts in foil-lined, 8-inch square pan. Sprinkle water over breasts. Sprinkle with gravy mix, salt, and pepper and dot with margarine. Seal foil tightly over birds. Roast 1 hour. Makes 3 to 4 servings.

Wally's Sauerkraut Goose

From Wally Jorgensen of Spirit Lake, Iowa

1 goose, skinned or plucked
Margarine
Mrs. Dash seasoning
Celery salt
Onion salt
Lawry's seasoned salt
4 or 5 slices bacon
1 large can of sauerkraut, drained

Preheat oven to 300 degrees. Place goose in roaster. Rub breast with margarine. Sprinkle lightly with Mrs. Dash, celery salt, onion salt, and Lawry's seasoned salt. Lay bacon on goose. Stuff small amount of kraut into body cavity, then cover breast with remaining kraut. Cover pan and roast until goose is tender, usually 4 to 5 hours, depending on age of bird. Take lid off roaster for last 20 minutes to brown kraut and goose. Makes 4 to 6 servings.

Fruited Venison Steak

1 pound venison, cut into ¾-inch-thick steaks
1 cup white wine
Vegetable oil
1 cup dry red wine
1 teaspoon sugar
1 cup frozen blueberries
1 tablespoon butter

Place steaks in single layer in dish and add white wine to cover. Cover with plastic wrap and refrigerate at least 1 hour or as long as 2 days. Remove meat from marinade. Place thin film of oil in bottom of heavy skillet large enough to hold meat in single layer. Heat on medium-high until hot. Add meat and cook 2 minutes. Turn meat and reduce heat to medium-low. Cook 2 minutes more. Turn meat and cook 3 minutes longer or until medium-rare. Remove meat to plate and cover with another plate to keep warm. Increase heat to high and add red wine. Boil, scraping browned bits from skillet, until wine is reduced to 1 cup. Add sugar, blueberries, and collected juices from steaks. Continue boiling until wine is reduced to ½ cup. Remove from heat and stir in butter. Spoon sauce and berries over meat. Makes 4 servings.

Rosemary's Rabbit

2 whole rabbits, cleaned and skinned
2 teaspoons salt
3 tablespoons fresh rosemary leaves
½ cup olive oil
½ cup onion, diced
2 garlic cloves, peeled and crushed
2 cups dry white wine
1 cup fresh or canned tomatoes, peeled, seeded, and chopped
8 sprigs fresh rosemary
1 quart chicken stock

1 teaspoon freshly ground black pepper
¼ cup flour
¼ cup cold water

Preheat oven to 325 degrees. Rinse rabbit. Pat dry with paper towels. Cut rabbit in half lengthwise through backbone. Combine salt and rosemary leaves and rub generously over rabbit pieces.

Heat oil in large, oven-proof skillet over medium heat. Brown rabbit halves, two pieces at a time, until golden brown on both sides. Remove rabbit, reduce heat under skillet, and add onion and garlic. Cook gently, stirring occasionally, 4 minutes. Return rabbit to skillet. Add wine, tomatoes, rosemary sprigs, chicken stock, and pepper. Place lid partially over skillet and roast in oven 1½ hours or until rabbit is tender. Remove rabbit from skillet and let cool slightly.

While rabbit is cooling, place skillet on top of stove and return to simmer over high heat. Combine flour and water and add to sauce, stirring with whisk. Reduce heat and simmer 15 to 20 minutes, until sauce thickens. Partially debone rabbit if desired: remove breast bone, back bone, and thigh bone, and separate the breast from thigh/leg piece. Return semiboneless rabbit to skillet over low heat for 10 minutes.

To serve, arrange a breast and thigh/leg section on each plate, ladle sauce over pieces, and garnish with additional fresh rosemary sprigs. Serve with roasted vegetables. Makes 4 servings.

Squirrel

From Doyle Adams of Indianola, Iowa

OLD SQUIRREL
1 squirrel, cleaned and skinned
Barbecue sauce

Put squirrel in pot. Cover with water and bring to boil. Reduce heat and simmer until meat falls off bone. Cut meat into bite-sized pieces. Place pieces in saucepan and top with generous amount of barbecue sauce. Cover and simmer 20 minutes.

YOUNG OR OLD SQUIRREL

1 squirrel, cleaned and skinned
1 cup sour cream
2 medium onions, chopped

Preheat oven to 350 degrees. Bone and cut squirrel into bite-sized pieces and brown in frying pan. Put pieces in casserole. Mix sour cream and onions and spread over squirrel. Roast 1 hour for young squirrel, longer for older one.

Extras

Caribbean-Style Chutney

From Mimi Gormezano of Iowa City, Iowa

1 cup chopped fresh pineapple
1 cup chopped fresh papaya
1 cup chopped fresh mango
1 cup chopped banana
Juice from 2 limes
About 2 tablespoons finely minced chili peppers (or more, to taste)
Grated, unsweetened coconut, to taste (optional)

Combine ingredients and let sit 1 hour or longer (will get hotter on standing). Serve as side dish for fish, poultry, or pork. Makes 4 cups.

Peachy Plum Chutney

1¼ cups sugar
1 cup cider vinegar
2 tablespoons fresh ginger, minced
2 large cloves garlic, minced
2½ pounds pitted and chopped fresh plums
2 pounds peeled, pitted, and chopped fresh peaches
2 cups raisins
2 teaspoons mustard seeds
¾ teaspoon salt
½ teaspoon cinnamon
¼ teaspoon cayenne pepper

Combine sugar, vinegar, ginger, and garlic and boil 10 minutes. Add remaining ingredients and boil 40 to 50 minutes or until thick, stirring frequently the last 10 minutes to prevent sticking and scorching. Ladle into 6 hot, sterilized half-pint jars, leaving ½-inch headroom. Adjust caps. Process 15 minutes in boiling water bath. Makes 6 half pints.

Tomato Chutney

1 pound tomatoes, blanched, peeled, and chopped, or
 1 pound canned peeled tomatoes, undrained
1 medium onion, finely chopped
1-inch piece fresh ginger, finely chopped
¾ cup pitted dates
⅔ cup raisins
⅔ cup currants
1 teaspoon cayenne pepper
1 teaspoon salt
4 tablespoons vegetable oil
1 teaspoon mustard seeds

Place all ingredients except oil and mustard seeds in saucepan and bring to boil, stirring occasionally. Reduce heat and simmer, uncovered, 1½ to 2 hours or until chutney is thick. Meanwhile, heat oil in small frying pan. Add mustard seeds and fry, covered, until they stop popping. Remove pan from heat and tip contents into saucepan with other ingredients. Stir to mix. Refrigerate. Serve with meat or fish.

Food pages take a look at food-related happenings around the state. In 1989, for example, a page reflected on food trends illustrated by the changes in the Meredith Test Kitchen in Des Moines over the past sixty years. Another food page noted recipes from the new Terrace Hill cookbook. Proceeds from sales of that book go to continuing preservation efforts at the governor's Victorian mansion.

Corn Relish

From Judy Arnold of Indianola, Iowa

10 cups corn
1 cup chopped green bell pepper
1 cup chopped red bell pepper
1 cup chopped onion
1 tablespoon salt
1½ cups sugar
2½ tablespoons mustard seeds
1 teaspoon celery seeds
2½ cups white vinegar
2 cups water

Combine ingredients; boil 15 minutes. Pack into hot, sterilized jars, leaving ½-inch headroom. Process in boiling water bath according to USDA canning guidelines. Makes 8 half pints.

Cranberry Salsa

Just a little different

1 cup fresh or frozen cranberries
1 green, yellow, or red bell pepper, cored, seeded, and roughly chopped
1 fresh jalapeño pepper, seeds and veins removed, minced
½ medium red onion, peeled and roughly chopped
½ cup fresh cilantro or parsley
4 ounces (⅔ of 6-ounce can) frozen orange juice concentrate, thawed

Place ingredients in blender or food processor fitted with metal blade; process until ingredients are coarsely chopped. Use to accompany hot or cold meat and poultry or to top such specialties as chicken tacos, turkey enchiladas, or quesadillas. May be stored in airtight, non-aluminum container for up to 2 weeks. Makes 3 cups.

Mango Salsa

Especially good with grilled chicken or fish

3 mangoes, peeled and chopped
1 large red bell pepper, cored, seeded, and chopped
3 tablespoons cilantro, chopped
2 teaspoons chives, chopped
1 tablespoon olive oil
Coarse black pepper
1 small onion, minced
3 tablespoons rice vinegar
2 tablespoons sugar
1 large avocado, peeled and chopped
Salt and pepper to taste

In glass or plastic bowl, combine mangoes, red pepper, cilantro, chives, oil, and several grinds of black pepper. In stainless steel, enamel, or nonstick saucepan, put onion, vinegar, and sugar and bring to boil; cook 1 minute. Remove from heat and cool a couple of minutes, then pour over mango mixture and toss. Cool a few minutes before tossing with avocado. Salt and pepper to taste and refrigerate.

Squash Relish

Peel of 1 orange (orange part only)
2 tablespoons mixed pickling spice
⅔ cup firmly packed light brown sugar
2 teaspoons salt
4 cups water
⅓ cup white vinegar
2 cups (2 large) sliced red onions
1 cup sweet red, green, or yellow bell pepper (about 1 large) cut into ¾-inch chunks
3 pounds (about 10 cups) zucchini and/or yellow squash, sliced ¼ inch thick

Use vegetable peeler to remove orange peel. Place pickling spice and orange peel on square of double thickness cheesecloth; pull up ends, tie with a string, and set aside. In stainless steel, enamel, or nonstick pan, combine brown sugar, salt, water, vinegar, and reserved spice bag. Bring to boil, reduce heat, and simmer, covered, 10 minutes to blend flavors; cool slightly. Add onions and pepper; simmer 2 minutes. Add squash; simmer until squash is nearly crisp-tender, about 2 minutes. Discard spice bag. Remove from heat. Place relish in covered containers; refrigerate 24 hours before serving. To freeze, place in 5 (2-cup) plastic containers, covering vegetables with liquid and filling to within ½ inch of top. Cover and freeze up to 6 months. Defrost in refrigerator, about 24 hours. Serve in turkey sandwiches or with meat and fish salads or seafood. Makes 10 cups.

Tomatillo Salsa

From Linda Hodges of Ames, Iowa

12 tomatillos
3 ounces olive oil
1 large onion, peeled and sliced
3 jalapeño peppers, stems and seeds removed, finely chopped
2 cloves garlic, finely minced
½ cup chicken stock

¼ cup fresh cilantro leaves, packed
Juice from 1½ limes
Salt

Remove tomatillo husks, wash well, halve, and set aside. Heat heavy-bottomed skillet over medium-high heat. Add oil. When small wisps of smoke appear, add onion and sauté briefly. Add jalapeños and garlic. Sauté until onion is translucent. Add tomatillos and chicken stock and bring mixture to boil. Remove from heat and pour into shallow container to cool. When cooled, pour mixture into food processor fitted with steel blade. Add cilantro and lime juice. Pulse motor on and off until mixture is uniformly coarse. Do not puree. Correct seasoning with salt. Salsa may be made a day in advance and refrigerated. Makes about 1½ cups.

May I drop a name? For several holiday seasons, Gene Shalit, critic-at-large on the *Today* show, called for suggestions on where to order a festive gift basket of gourmet foods for his boss, Michael Gartner, then president of NBC News. Gartner returned to his native Des Moines on the weekends, so Shalit wanted the basket delivered to his home.

One time I suggested Brandywine House, a gourmet gift shop. "Do you think they'd deliver?" Shalit asked.

"Oh, sure," I answered. "The shop is only a little more than a mile from Gartner's house. I'm sure there's no problem."

Long silence on the other end.

"Excuse me. You *know* where Gartner lives?" asked the critic.

"Of course. He was formerly our boss, too, you know," I said. "This is a big small town. Sure, I know where he lives."

Shalit was unbelieving. "In New York, no one knows where anyone else lives."

A few days later a gift bag arrived at the *Register*—one of Mrs. Prindible's huge decorated apples—to be shared with the newsroom foodies. "Thanks for your help. A big apple from the Big Apple." The card still holds a prominent spot on my refrigerator door.

Tropical Fruit Pico Relish

From Michael's Restaurant, Fort Worth, Texas

1 cup fresh tomatoes, seeded and diced small
1 cup white onions, diced small
2 tablespoons fresh jalapeño, finely chopped
1 cup cantaloupe, diced small
1 cup mango, diced small
1 cup papaya, diced small
1 cup fresh cilantro, chopped
½ cup fresh lime juice
2 tablespoons sugar
1 tablespoon salt
1 tablespoon pepper
2 tablespoons butter

Mix all ingredients except butter and marinate 2 hours before cooking. In skillet over medium flame, heat butter until almost brown. Add pico mixture and simmer 3 to 4 minutes until thoroughly warmed. Fruit should have texture. (If you overcook, fruit will break down and become mushy.) This is a wonderful accompaniment to fish; time relish procedure so it will be ready just as fish is done. Makes 4 servings.

Pineapple Salsa

1 large fresh pineapple
½ cup diced red bell pepper
3 tablespoons minced red onion
3 tablespoons minced fresh basil
1 tablespoon balsamic vinegar
4 teaspoons white wine vinegar
¼ teaspoon red pepper flakes
⅛ teaspoon salt

Twist crown from pineapple. Cut pineapple lengthwise in quarters. Cut fruit from shells. Trim off core. Cut fruit into bite-sized pieces. Measure 3 cups for recipe; refrigerate remaining for later use. Combine pineapple with remaining ingredients. Cover; refrigerate 1 hour. Serve over hamburgers or chicken. Makes 10 servings.

Green Tomato Piccalilli

Good end-of-garden relish

3 medium green tomatoes, chopped
1 teaspoon salt
2 ears corn, shucked
1 cup white vinegar
1 cup sugar
¼ teaspoon ground cloves
¼ teaspoon ground cinnamon
⅛ teaspoon Tabasco sauce
¼ to ½ cup chopped onion
1 red bell pepper, seeded and finely chopped

Rub tomato slices with salt and let stand overnight, covered, in refrigerator. To remove excess moisture, press tomatoes between pieces of paper towel. Bring large pan of water to boil; add corn and cook 3 minutes. Drain and cut kernels from cob. In medium saucepan, combine vinegar, sugar, cloves, cinnamon, and Tabasco. Bring to boil, stirring to dissolve sugar. Combine tomatoes, corn, onion, and pepper. Add hot vinegar-sugar syrup and mix well. Cool, cover, and refrigerate until ready to serve. Makes about 3½ cups.

Artichoke Pasta Sauce

1 (6-ounce) jar marinated artichoke hearts
1 cup thinly sliced onion
1 large clove garlic, minced
1 (14½-ounce) can whole peeled tomatoes and juice
1 (6-ounce) can tomato paste
1 cup water
2 tablespoons chopped fresh basil or 2 teaspoons dried basil

Drain artichoke marinade into 2-quart saucepan; quarter artichokes and set aside. Add onion and garlic to marinade. Cook over medium heat until onion is tender. Drain juice from tomatoes into marinade. Coarsely chop tomatoes and add along with tomato paste, water, and basil. Add artichokes and continue cooking until bubbly. Serve over cooked pasta. Makes 4 servings.

Barbecue Sauce

From Eliot Nusbaum of Carlisle, Iowa

2 parts taco sauce (medium or hot)
2 parts ketchup
2 parts brown sugar
1 part liquid smoke
1 tablespoon garlic powder
½ teaspoon crushed red pepper

Mix ingredients together. Good as marinade, barbecue sauce, and mixed with baked beans. It's handy to use ½ or 1 cup measures as the "parts."

NOTE: The longer this sits, the hotter it gets. If you double recipe, do not double taco sauce or red pepper flakes.

Medium White Sauce

2 tablespoons butter
2 tablespoons flour
1 cup milk
1 scant teaspoon salt
Dash of white or black pepper

Melt butter over very low heat (or in double boiler). Add flour and blend until smooth. Add milk, stirring constantly, and cook until sauce is thickened and smooth. Add salt and pepper. Cover and cook 5 to 7 minutes over low heat. Makes 1 cup.

NOTE: If you are making larger quantities of white sauce, heat milk before adding.

Sesame Marinade

From Tom McCartan of Pocahontas, Iowa

½ cup soy sauce
4 teaspoons brown sugar
4 tablespoons vegetable oil
4 teaspoons sesame seeds
2 tablespoons minced garlic or garlic salt

Mix ingredients. Use as marinade for grilled beef. Marinate meat at least 4 hours or overnight. Makes about ¾ cup of sauce.

Fresh Herb Vinegar

2 sprigs fresh tarragon
2 sprigs fresh dill
1 bunch chives
Fresh basil
Fresh parsley
Other leafy herbs of your choice
3 cups white wine vinegar

Put herbs in bottle. Add vinegar to fill. Cap and let steep 2 weeks. Makes 3 cups.

Fresh Rosemary Vinegar

2 to 3 sprigs fresh rosemary
6 garlic cloves
Whole black peppercorn
3 cups white wine vinegar

Combine ingredients. Cap and let steep 2 weeks. Makes 3 cups.

Roasted Red Bell Peppers

Rinse peppers; pat dry. Place whole peppers on cooking grate. Grill peppers, turning every 5 minutes until charred evenly on all sides. Watch carefully. Remove peppers from grill and place in paper bag; close tightly. Let stand 10 to 15 minutes. Remove peppers from bag; peel away charred skins. Cut off tops and remove seeds. Use for garnish on any barbecued dish.

Dried Tomatoes

2 pounds Roma tomatoes
Salt to taste
Freshly ground black pepper
Chopped herbs of your choice (such as oregano or thyme)
Olive oil

Preheat oven to 200 degrees. Wash tomatoes under running cold water and drain until dry. Cut tomatoes in half lengthwise and place on large cake rack atop cookie sheet. Season with salt, pepper, and herbs. Place cookie sheet on upper rack of oven and prop open oven door slightly with wooden spoon to create ventilation.

Allow tomatoes to dry until they have shrunk by about half but are still pliable, about 8 hours. Remove from oven and allow to cool to room temperature. Lightly pack in sterilized glass jars; cover with oil. Or refrigerate in zip-top plastic bags. Makes about 1 pound.

Rhubarb-Strawberry Jam

1 quart fully ripe strawberries
1½ pounds fully ripe rhubarb
½ cup water
6 cups sugar

1 box (1¾ ounces) Sure Jell fruit pectin
½ teaspoon butter or margarine

Boil 7 (1-cup) jars for 10 minutes on rack in large pot filled with water. Place flat lids in saucepan with water; bring to boil; remove from heat. Let jars and lids stand in hot water until ready to fill. Drain well before filling.

Stem and thoroughly crush strawberries, one layer at a time. Measure 2¼ cups into 6- or 8-quart pot. Finely chop rhubarb; do not peel. Place in 2-quart saucepan; add water. Bring to boil. Reduce heat; cover and simmer 2 minutes or until rhubarb is soft. Measure 1¾ cups; add to strawberries. Measure sugar into separate bowl. Scrape extra sugar from cup with spatula to level for exact measure. Stir pectin into fruit in sauce pot. Add butter. Place on high heat; bring to full rolling boil, stirring constantly. Immediately stir in all sugar. Return to full rolling boil and boil 1 minute, stirring constantly. Remove from heat; skim foam with metal spoon. Ladle quickly into prepared jars, filling to within ⅛ inch of tops. Wipe jar rims and threads. Cover with two-piece lids. Tighten bands. Invert jars 5 minutes, then turn upright. After jars cool, check seals. Makes about 7 (1-cup) jars.

NOTE: It is important to measure sugar and fruit exactly; do not change amounts or jam will not set properly.

Strawberry Freezer Jam

2 cups strawberries
4 cups sugar
2 boxes powdered fruit pectin
1½ cups water

Mash berries and mix thoroughly with sugar. Set aside. Stir fruit pectin into water in saucepan. Bring to boil, stirring constantly. Boil 1 minute. Add berries and stir until sugar is completely dissolved. Pour into clean, dry containers, filling to within ½ inch of tops. Immediately cover with tight lids. Let stand at room temperature overnight. Store in freezer until opened; then store in refrigerator. Makes about 4 (8-ounce) containers.

One-Dish Meals

Double-Crust Pizza Casserole

From Roy Ney of Des Moines, Iowa

CRUST
3 cups flour
3 cups instant mashed potatoes (dry, not prepared)
1¼ cups milk
1¼ cups melted butter

FILLING
1 pound ground beef
1 pound bulk Italian sausage
1 large onion, coarsely chopped
1 (6-ounce) can tomato sauce
1 (6-ounce) can ripe pitted olives, drained and halved
1 (6-ounce) can tomato paste
1 (1.3-ounce) package sloppy joe seasoning mix
¼ teaspoon garlic powder
1½ cups shredded mozzarella cheese

Preheat oven to 425 degrees. Combine crust ingredients and set aside. In skillet, brown beef, sausage, and onion; drain. Stir in tomato sauce, olives, tomato paste, seasoning mix, and garlic powder. Press half of crust mixture into bottom and up sides of a greased 13 × 9-inch baking dish. Spread filling over crust; top with cheese. Roll remaining crust into 15 × 11-inch rectangle on waxed paper. Invert over filling and trim edges. Turn edges under and crimp. Bake 30 to 35 minutes or until crust is golden brown. Let stand 5 minutes before serving.

Make-Your-Own Pizza

See Pizza Party for Eight, p. 260.

A national food conference put on by Kraft came to Decorah in the spring of 1994. Why Decorah? Because it's an ethnic spot, rich in Norwegian heritage, not particularly close to a large city. Trackers of national food trends wanted to see if such a pocket would naturally follow major trends. Meeting in the Clarksville Diner, which had been moved from the East Coast and restored, food editors from around the country mingled with local "foodies" and found that, indeed, Decorah fell in line with national trends. Yes, healthful foods are important, but "pleasure revenge," as they call it there, is alive and well, too. People are only too happy to treat themselves to small indulgences. Pizza is pervasive, showing up in many forms in many places. And ethnic boundaries are falling quickly, creating uncounted new examples of "fusion food." One Decorah mother often serves Mexican tacos in Norwegian lefse, for example.

Mediterranean Pizza

CRUST

1 (¼-ounce) package of dry yeast
2 tablespoons sugar
1 cup lukewarm water
4 cups flour
Pinch of salt
2 large eggs, beaten
2 tablespoons virgin olive oil

TOPPINGS

Cornmeal for dusting pizza
½ cup chopped fresh basil, divided
2 tablespoons olive oil
½ cup mozzarella cheese, grated
¼ cup capers, drained

½ cup oven-dried tomatoes, diced
½ cup porcini mushrooms, chopped
¼ cup Parmesan cheese, finely grated

CRUST: In small bowl, combine yeast, sugar, and water. Let set until foamy. In food processor with plastic dough blade or regular blade, combine flour and salt. Mix in eggs, then yeast mixture, until ball forms. Work just until dough pulls away from side of bowl, then add oil. Remove dough immediately to oiled bowl, cover with clean cloth, and allow to rise in dry, warm place until doubled, about 45 minutes. Punch down; allow to double again, about 20 minutes. Form into 5 balls.

Lightly flour dough and counter. Roll dough into very thin 9-inch circles. Proceed with toppings and bake. Or put between waxed paper sheets in the refrigerator until needed, up to 3 days.

TOPPINGS: Preheat oven to 550 degrees. Dust bottom of pizza crust with cornmeal. Combine ¼ cup basil with oil and spread across top of dough. Cover with mozzarella. Distribute capers, tomatoes, and mushrooms over cheese. Place on cookie sheet. Bake 8 to 12 minutes, until crust is golden. Remove from oven, sprinkle with Parmesan and remaining ¼ cup basil. Makes one 9-inch pizza.

Cheese and Herb Quesadillas

Have guests serve themselves

1 package (10-inch) flour tortillas
8 ounces grated cheese (such as Monterey Jack, Cheddar, or Colby)
1 cup assorted fresh herbs (such as cilantro, basil, chives, and parsley), minced
2 small tomatoes, thinly sliced
¼ cup red bell pepper, chopped
¼ cup green bell pepper, chopped
Salsa and sour cream
Shredded romaine, iceberg, or leaf lettuce

Lightly toast each flour tortilla directly over gas burner or in dry, well-seasoned skillet until light brown. Wrap in clean towel to keep warm. Put tortillas and all ingredients in small bowls on table. Have guests assemble quesadillas. Put 3 at a time on microwave-safe plate. Microwave on high just until cheese is warm and melted, about 1½ minutes. Fold in half to eat. Makes 6 servings.

Cheese Tortillas

Easy, hearty casserole

1 (16-ounce) container low-fat cottage cheese
1 cup whole kernel corn
¾ cup (6 ounces) shredded sharp Cheddar cheese, divided
¼ cup sliced green onions
2 tablespoons chopped cilantro
½ teaspoon Mexican seasoning
6 (6-inch) flour tortillas
1 cup salsa

Preheat oven to 350 degrees. Mix cottage cheese, corn, ¼ cup Cheddar cheese, onions, cilantro, and seasoning. Spoon about ½ cup cheese-corn mixture down center of each tortilla; roll up. Arrange, seam-side down, in greased 13 × 9-inch baking dish. Top with salsa and remaining Cheddar cheese. Bake 30 minutes. Makes 6 servings.

Vegetable Tostadas

Healthful Mexican fare

2 tablespoons safflower oil, divided
2 (16-ounce) cans pinto beans, drained and rinsed
1 tablespoon chili powder
1 teaspoon ground cumin
1 (16-ounce) jar medium-thick salsa, divided
8 (6-inch) tortillas
2 cups shredded romaine or iceberg lettuce

Preheat oven to 400 degrees. In medium saucepan, heat 1 tablespoon oil until hot. Add pinto beans; cook and stir 3 to 4 minutes. Stir in chili powder and cumin. Mash beans slightly. Add ¾ cup salsa; bring to boil. Reduce heat and simmer, uncovered, until bean mixture is thickened, 5 to 10 minutes, stirring occasionally. Meanwhile, place tortillas in single layer on large baking sheet. Brush lightly with remaining 1 tablespoon oil. Bake until crisp, 5 to 6 minutes. To serve, divide beans among crisped tortillas. Top with shredded lettuce and remaining ¼ cup salsa. Makes 4 servings.

Top-Secret Tamale Pie

From Jennifer Phelps of Carlisle, Iowa

1 pound beef chuck
1 pound pork
1 teaspoon chili powder
1 large onion, finely chopped
2 cloves garlic, minced
Salt and pepper to taste
1 cup yellow cornmeal
1 cup water
1 (12-ounce) can cream-style corn
1 (12-ounce) can whole kernel corn
1 (6-ounce) can tomato paste
1 (8-ounce) can ripe olives
1 cup Cheddar cheese, shredded

Preheat oven to 350 degrees. Dice meat and simmer 30 minutes in water to cover. Add chili powder, onion, garlic, salt, and pepper. Simmer 30 minutes. Moisten cornmeal in water. Add to meat. Stir in corn, tomato paste, and ripe olives. Transfer to large casserole and bake, uncovered, 1½ hours, stirring occasionally and adding more water if needed. Cover with cheese and return to oven until cheese is melted, about 10 minutes. Makes 6 to 8 servings.

Crab-Broccoli Casserole

An easy put-together

2 teaspoons vegetable oil
1 tablespoon onion, finely chopped
1 tablespoon flour
¼ teaspoon hot pepper sauce
Dash of pepper
½ cup skim milk
1 (6-ounce) can crab meat, drained and cartilage removed
1½ cups frozen chopped broccoli
Paprika, for garnish

Combine oil and onion in 4-cup glass measure. Microwave on high 45 seconds. Stir in flour, hot pepper sauce, and pepper. Gradually stir in milk. Microwave on high 1 to 2 minutes or until thickened, stirring every 30 seconds. Stir in crab meat. Place broccoli in 2 microwave-safe casseroles. Cover with plastic wrap. Microwave on high 1 to 2 minutes or until thawed, stirring once. Drain off liquid. Spoon crab meat mixture over broccoli. Sprinkle with paprika. Cover with plastic wrap. Microwave on medium (half power) 1½ minutes or until thoroughly heated. Makes 2 servings.

Farmhouse Potatoes 'n' Ham

5 or 6 large russet potatoes (about 2½ pounds), peeled and thinly sliced
¼ cup butter or margarine
3 tablespoons flour
1⅓ cups milk
2 teaspoons prepared mustard
⅓ cup sweet red onion, minced
1⅓ cups shredded Cheddar cheese, divided
1½ cups diced cooked ham
¼ teaspoon salt
⅛ teaspoon pepper
⅓ cup seasoned dry bread crumbs

Preheat oven to 350 degrees. Arrange sliced potatoes in 2- to 2½-quart oblong oven-safe casserole and set aside. Put butter in 4-cup glass measure or microwave-safe bowl. Microwave on high about 45 seconds to melt. Blend in flour, milk, and mustard. Microwave on high 3 minutes. Stir and add onion. Microwave on high until sauce thickens. Add 1 cup cheese and stir until melted. Fold in ham, salt and pepper. Pour sauce over potatoes. Sprinkle with remaining ⅓ cup cheese and top with bread crumbs. Bake 50 to 60 minutes, until potatoes are tender. Makes 6 to 8 servings.

"Smart chefs realize that the easiest cookbook to use is the Yellow Pages and the handiest appliance in the kitchen is the telephone. With it, you can turn out more delicious meals than with your oven, your broiler, your blender, and all your pots and pans combined."—*Miss Piggy's Guide to Life*

Spinach Pie

A Greek specialty

2 pounds spinach
½ pound feta cheese, crumbled
½ pound cottage cheese
Salt and white pepper
6 eggs, separated
¾ pound butter, melted
½ pound phyllo pastry sheets

Preheat oven to 350 degrees. Clean and chop spinach and place in large mixing bowl. Add feta cheese, cottage cheese, salt, and pepper. Add egg yolks and mix thoroughly. Beat egg whites until stiff and fold into spinach mixture. Grease 13 × 9-inch pan and place 6 phyllo sheets in pan, brushing each with melted butter as you stack them. Spread spinach mixture evenly over phyllo and cover with 6 more individually buttered phyllo sheets. Bake about 1 hour or until golden brown. Cut into squares and serve hot or cold. Makes 12 servings.

Turkey-Stuffed Squash

Good dish for nippy winter days

2 acorn squashes, each about 1¼ pounds
½ cup chopped onion
1 tablespoon vegetable oil
¾ pound ground turkey
1 cup red cooking apple, finely chopped
1 tablespoon flour
3 tablespoons reduced-sodium soy sauce
¼ cup seedless raisins

Cut squashes in half lengthwise; discard seeds and fiber. Place cut-side down in microwave-safe baking dish; cover with plastic wrap. Microwave on high 4 minutes; turn squashes over and rotate dish. Microwave on high 4 minutes more or until squashes are tender yet firm. Meanwhile, in large skillet, sauté onion in hot oil over high heat until translucent. Add turkey and apple; stir over medium heat about 5 minutes or until turkey is no longer pink. Sprinkle flour over meat mixture; stir to blend. Gradually stir in soy sauce; cook and stir until slightly thickened. Stir in raisins; remove from heat. Fill each squash half with equal amount of turkey mixture. Cover loosely and microwave on high 1 minute or until filling is heated through. Makes 4 servings.

Zucchini Lasagne

A healthful approach

9 lasagne noodles
½ pound zucchini, cut into ⅛-inch-thick slices, divided
1 (15-ounce) carton ricotta cheese
8 ounces shredded mozzarella cheese, divided
1 tablespoon soy sauce
½ teaspoon ground oregano, crumbled

SAUCE
1 pound ground turkey or chicken
2 cloves pressed garlic, divided
2 tablespoons olive oil, divided
1 medium onion, chopped
2 pounds Italian plum tomatoes, coarsely chopped
¼ cup soy sauce

Preheat oven to 375 degrees. Cook lasagne noodles according to package directions. Drain and set aside. Cook zucchini slices until crisp-tender. Set aside. Combine ricotta, 4 ounces mozzarella, soy sauce, and oregano.

SAUCE: Cook ground turkey or chicken with 1 clove garlic in 1 tablespoon oil until no longer pink; remove from pan and set aside. In same pan, put onion, 1 clove garlic, and 1 tablespoon oil and cook until onion is translucent. Stir in tomatoes and soy sauce. Cover; simmer 10 minutes, stirring occasionally to break up tomatoes. Uncover and simmer 15 additional minutes. Stir in cooked turkey; simmer 3 minutes.

ASSEMBLY: In 13 × 9-inch greased baking pan, place 3 lasagne noodles side by side. Spread half of cheese mixture and half of tomato sauce over noodles. Arrange zucchini in single layer over sauce. Repeat with layer of noodles, cheese, and sauce. Top with layer of noodles. Sprinkle remaining 4 ounces mozzarella over noodles. Bake 35 minutes. Remove from oven and let stand 10 minutes before serving. Makes 12 servings.

Vegetable Lasagne

A meatless version

3 tablespoons margarine or butter
⅓ cup plus 1 tablespoon flour
½ teaspoon pepper
3 cups skim milk
1 (14-ounce) can asparagus, drained, or ½ pound fresh asparagus, steamed, cut into ½-inch pieces
2 cups frozen Mediterranean vegetables, cooked until crisp-tender
4 no-boil lasagne noodles, dry
1 tablespoon chopped fresh parsley

Melt butter in saucepan over medium heat; stir in flour. Add pepper; heat 1 minute. Stir in milk; continue stirring until mixture boils. Boil 1 minute. Stir in asparagus pieces. Spread about ½ cup sauce on bottom of 9 × 5-inch loaf pan. Cover with 1 dry lasagne noodle. Cover noodle with ½ cup sauce. Sprinkle with ½ cup vegetables. Repeat layers of noodles, sauce, and vegetables three more times, ending with sauce on top. Sprinkle with parsley. Makes 3 to 4 servings.

CONVENTIONAL OVEN: Preheat oven to 350 degrees. Cover lasagne with foil. Bake 20 to 25 minutes. Let stand 5 minutes before serving.

MICROWAVE: Use microwave-safe loaf pan. Cover with plastic wrap. Cook on high 15 minutes, turning dish twice during cooking.

NOTE: Fresh zucchini, carrots, cauliflower, Italian beans, lima beans, and red bell peppers may be substituted for frozen Mediterranean vegetables.

Turned-on Tuna Casserole

From Jennifer Phelps of Carlisle, Iowa

1 (6-ounce) can tuna
1 clove garlic, minced
2 medium zucchini, thinly sliced
1 medium onion, chopped
4 tablespoons butter, divided
1 (8-ounce) can tomato sauce
8 ounces American cheese, grated
Salt and pepper
4 slices bread, cubed

Preheat oven to 350 degrees. Drain tuna and add garlic. Sauté zucchini and onion in 2 tablespoons butter until tender and most of excess liquid has evaporated. Transfer to buttered casserole. Add tuna and mix. Pour tomato sauce evenly over tuna and zucchini. Top with cheese. Salt and pepper to taste. Add layer of bread cubes; dot with remaining 2 tablespoons butter. Bake 25 to 30 minutes or until cheese is melted. Makes 4 servings.

George's Spaghetti

From the late George Goetz of Davenport, Iowa
Definitely not Italian, but really good

1½ pounds ground round
1 to 2 tablespoons peanut oil
2 medium onions, cut into chunks
1 small green bell pepper, cut into chunks
8 Brazil nuts or ½ cup white peanuts
4 (10½-ounce) cans tomato sauce
3 tablespoons ketchup
4 garlic cloves, crushed
1½ teaspoons Worcestershire sauce
3 tablespoons soy sauce
Freshly ground black pepper

2 teaspoons angostura bitters
¼ teaspoon paprika
½ teaspoon celery salt
2 tablespoons Parmesan cheese, grated
Chunk of blue cheese, size of walnut
½ teaspoon dried basil leaves, pulverized in hand
3 tablespoons fresh parsley, finely chopped
Pinch of baking soda
¾ to 1 cup red table wine

In skillet, brown meat in oil just until it begins to brown. Put onions, pepper, and nuts in food processor and pulse until chopped but not pureed. Add onion mixture to meat and cook on medium heat until onions begin to brown. Remove from heat and set aside.

In 4-quart nonaluminum pot, put remaining ingredients except baking soda and red wine. Bring to boil. Stir in meat mixture from skillet. Do not cover. Reduce heat to simmer. Add baking soda after first 30 minutes. Continue cooking 3 to 4 hours, stirring every 15 minutes and adding 1 tablespoon red table wine with each stirring, until grease covers top. Skim grease from sauce. Taste and adjust seasonings by adding bitters, Worcestershire, soy sauce, or salt. Serve over spaghetti cooked al dente. Makes about 8 servings.

Baked Country Stew

Make it and bake it

2 pounds beef stew meat
3 or 4 potatoes
3 or 4 carrots
2 ribs celery
3 small onions
1 (28-ounce) can tomatoes
¼ cup water
5 tablespoons Minute Tapioca
2 tablespoons Worcestershire sauce
1 tablespoon brown sugar
1 teaspoon salt
½ teaspoon pepper
½ teaspoon ground allspice
¼ teaspoon ground marjoram
¼ teaspoon ground thyme
1 bay leaf
½ cup chopped fresh parsley

Preheat oven to 300 degrees. Cut meat into bite-sized pieces. Peel and cut potatoes into pieces a bit larger than meat. Clean carrots, celery, and onions and cut into 1-inch pieces. In large, heavy roasting pan or ceramic slow-cooker pot, combine all ingredients except parsley. Bake, covered, 5 hours without stirring. Add parsley just before serving. Makes 8 servings.

Beef and Black Bean Chili

Wonderfully unusual

2 teaspoons vegetable oil
1 pound lean ground beef
1 medium onion, chopped
1 large clove garlic, minced

2 (16-ounce) cans stewed tomatoes, with liquid
3 to 4 teaspoons chili powder
½ teaspoon ground cumin
¼ teaspoon pepper
2 (15½-ounce) cans black beans
1 cup frozen corn kernels
½ cup shredded Monterey Jack cheese
Fresh cilantro, for garnish (optional)

Measure oil into 2½-quart microwave-safe casserole; tilt to coat bottom. Crumble beef into casserole, then add onion and garlic. Cover and microwave on high 4 to 6 minutes or until meat is no longer pink, stirring twice. Stir in tomatoes, chili powder, cumin, and pepper. Cover and microwave on high 2 minutes. Rinse beans in colander under cold running water; drain well. Stir beans and corn into casserole. Cover and microwave on medium (half power) 12 to 22 minutes, stirring twice. Top with cheese and let stand 5 minutes before serving. Garnish with sprigs of cilantro, if desired. Makes 4 to 6 servings.

Winning Chili

2 tablespoons bacon fat
1 large onion, chopped
3 pounds beef chuck, coarsely ground
3 cloves garlic, minced
4 tablespoons chili powder
1½ teaspoons ground cumin
½ teaspoon ground oregano
1 (8-ounce) can tomato sauce
2 cups water
1 tablespoon salt

Melt bacon fat in large, heavy pot over medium heat. Add onion and cook until translucent. Combine beef with garlic, chili powder, cumin, and oregano. Add meat mixture to onion. Break up any lumps with a fork and cook, stirring occasionally, about 30 minutes or until meat is evenly browned. Add tomato sauce, water, and salt. Bring to boil; lower heat and simmer, uncovered, 1 hour. Taste and adjust seasonings. Makes 8 servings.

Hearty Vegetable Beef Soup

From O'Hara's Steakhouse in Bedford, Iowa

2½ pounds thick-cut round steak
Black pepper
Garlic powder
4 cups diced potatoes
2 cups diced carrots
1½ cups diced celery
1½ cups diced onion
½ head diced green cabbage
4 quarts water
1 beef bouillon cube, mixed with ⅓ cup water
1 quart beef stock
1 teaspoon black pepper
1½ teaspoons garlic powder
½ teaspoon cayenne pepper
1 teaspoon Italian seasoning
1 (16-ounce) can tomatoes, diced

Preheat oven to 300 degrees. Season round steak liberally with black pepper and garlic powder. Place on rack in roasting pan and bake until meat thermometer registers 160 degrees. Reserve meat juices. Cut cooked meat into 1-inch pieces. In pot, put potatoes, carrots, celery, onion, and cabbage in water, bouillon, beef stock, and reserved meat juices; add seasonings and boil until vegetables are tender, 25 to 30 minutes. Reduce heat to low and add tomatoes and diced beef. Simmer 30 to 45 minutes, until flavors blend. Freezes well. Makes 2½ gallons.

Mediterranean Steak Soup

From Bill and Joyce Ludwig of Des Moines, Iowa

2 pounds round steak, cubed
¾ cup butter, divided
1 clove garlic, minced
2 cups mushrooms, sliced
2 cups onions, chopped
¼ cup bacon bits
2 cups carrots, sliced
2 cups celery, sliced
2 cups potatoes, sliced
8 cups water
1½ teaspoons salt
1½ teaspoons ground pepper
1 teaspoon leaf tarragon
1 (1-pound) can tomatoes
¾ cup flour
¼ cup Bovril or Jamison's liquid beef base or bouillon
2 tablespoons prepared horseradish
2 tablespoons Worcestershire sauce
1 tablespoon Accent seasoning
1 tablespoon ground allspice
⅛ cup fresh parsley, chopped
⅛ cup chives, chopped
1 (10-ounce) package frozen vegetables
4 ounces sherry

Cut meat in 1-inch cubes. Brown in large frying pan with ¼ cup butter and garlic. Remove meat and cook mushrooms, onion, and bacon bits in pan. Reserve mixture. Place carrots, celery, potatoes, water, salt, pepper, and tarragon in large kettle. Boil 5 minutes. Drain, saving liquid. Drain tomatoes and add liquid to vegetable liquid. Melt remaining ½ cup butter in large kettle. Stir in flour. Add onion-mushroom mixture. Gradually add vegetable liquid, stirring constantly. Add remaining ingredients except frozen vegetables and sherry. Combine meat, vegetables, and tomatoes with sauce. Cover and simmer 20 minutes. Add frozen vegetables and simmer 10 minutes. Serve with small amount of sherry in cordial glass. Makes 8 servings.

Apple-Cranberry Pancake Puff

It's yummy and pretty

½ cup water
¼ cup butter or margarine
½ cup buttermilk
½ cup pancake-waffle mix
2 eggs

FILLING
2 tart cooking apples, cut in thin wedges
2 tablespoons butter or margarine
½ cup pancake syrup
½ cup fresh cranberries or ¼ cup raisins
⅓ cup coarsely chopped pecans
½ teaspoon cinnamon
⅛ teaspoon ground nutmeg

Preheat oven to 400 degrees. Generously grease 9-inch glass pie plate. Bring water and butter to boil in medium saucepan. Stir buttermilk into pancake mix and add to water; beat vigorously until mixture leaves side of pan and forms ball. Remove from heat. Add eggs, one at a time, beating well after each addition. Spread batter evenly onto bottom and sides of pie plate. Bake 17 to 19 minutes or until golden brown. Fill immediately with fruit filling and cut into wedges to serve.

FILLING: In 10-inch skillet, cook apples in butter over medium heat 4 minutes or until almost tender, occasionally turning gently. Add remaining ingredients; cook 3 to 4 minutes or just until cranberries begin to pop. Makes 4 servings.

Pineapple French Toast with Ambrosia Salsa

AMBROSIA SALSA
1 (20-ounce) can pineapple tidbits or chunks in juice
1 cup fresh strawberry halves
¼ cup toasted shredded coconut
4 tablespoons sugar, divided

FRENCH TOAST
1 loaf (10 ounces) French or Italian bread slices
3 eggs

During the floods of 1993, food and how to prepare it without water became a real issue. In Des Moines, for example, there was no water for bathing, flushing, or laundering for twelve days. It took two weeks after that before drinking water was available. While most downtown offices had to take two weeks off, staffers at the *Register* worked overtime in sweltering conditions—no water for air conditioning, restroom facilities, even printing the newspaper itself.

One day a college friend, Barbara Durbin, who writes about food for the *Oregonian* in Portland, called. "I saw your stuff on national television news," she said.

"Oh, yeah," I said. "We're big news here. President Clinton is here, along with all the major TV anchors. Peter Jennings from ABC, Tom Brokaw from NBC, and Dan Rather from CBS. They're all here."

"No, I mean *your* stuff," she said. "Peter Jennings held up your food page and said, 'Wow. The paper here even tells people how to prepare food without water. Pretend you're camping, because you are.' "

I never saw it, but one of my colleagues was vacationing in Michigan and saw it, too. You never know what will trip someone's trigger.

1½ cups milk
1 teaspoon vanilla extract
¼ teaspoon salt
1 tablespoon butter

AMBROSIA SALSA: Drain pineapple; reserve ¾ cup juice and pineapple pieces separately. In small bowl, combine strawberries, coconut, reserved pineapple pieces, and 2 tablespoons sugar; set aside.

FRENCH TOAST: Cut bread into ¾-inch slices. In 15 × 10-inch jellyroll pan, arrange bread slices in single layer; set aside. In large bowl, beat eggs, milk, vanilla, salt, remaining 2 tablespoons sugar, and reserved pineapple juice; pour over bread, turning slices to coat completely. Cover and refrigerate overnight or until all liquid is absorbed, about 1½ hours.

In large skillet over medium heat, melt butter. Add bread a few pieces at a time and brown on both sides, turning once and adding more butter, if necessary. Top with Ambrosia Salsa. Makes 6 servings.

Monte Cristo Sandwich

Rich and wonderful

¼ cup apple butter
4 slices cinnamon-raisin bread
4 slices (1 ounce each) sharp Cheddar cheese
8 to 10 apple slices, ¼ inch thick
4 ounces thinly sliced smoked ham
2 eggs
2 tablespoons butter
Powdered sugar (optional)
Maple syrup (optional)

Spread half of apple butter on one side of 2 bread slices; top each with cheese slice, half the apple slices, half the ham, and remaining cheese slices. Spread remaining bread slices with rest of apple butter and close sandwiches. Beat eggs until blended. Carefully dip both sides of sandwiches into eggs. Melt butter in large, nonstick skillet over medium heat. Place sandwiches in skillet; cook each side until golden brown and sandwich is heated through. Cut into quarters. Sprinkle with powdered sugar and serve with maple syrup, if desired. Makes 2 sandwiches.

Albuquerque Eggs

From Michaela Karni of Albuquerque

½ cup butter or margarine
8 slices bread, cubed
8 eggs, beaten
2 cups milk
½ teaspoon salt
½ teaspoon pepper
1 or 2 (4½-ounce) cans chopped green chilies
4 to 6 ounces Monterey Jack cheese, grated

Melt butter in 13 × 9-inch baking pan. Spread bread cubes evenly in pan. Mix together eggs, milk, salt, and pepper and pour over bread. Pour undrained green chilies over top of egg mixture. Top with cheese. Cover and refrigerate at least 1 hour or overnight.

Preheat oven to 350 degrees. Bake casserole 30 to 45 minutes or until eggs are set. Makes up to 12 servings.

VARIATION: Cook ½ pound of bacon slices until crisp. Crumble into egg mixture before (or instead of) adding green chilies.

Eggs Florentine

See Back-to-Back Brunches for Twelve, p. 259.

Easy Omelet Variations

Eggs and butter; that's all you need to make a basic omelet

2 tablespoons butter
3 eggs

Melt butter in pan (either a covered frying pan or pan you can put in oven); beat eggs until foamy, then pour into pan and cover or place under broiler. When egg top is firm, omelet is done. (Expect broiler version to rise a few inches.)

What you do with the basic omelet is limited only by your imagination. Our two favorite recipes are chicken liver, onion, and mushroom (sauté in separate pan and spoon onto finished omelet) and Mexican Fiesta. For the Mexican Fiesta omelet, add hot peppers to egg batter. Once batter is in pan, top with sliced Cheddar cheese and proceed as above. Serve with sour cream and taco sauce.

Microwave Omelet

In a hurry?

1 tablespoon butter or margarine
4 large eggs
4 tablespoons water or 2 tablespoons water and 2 tablespoons milk
¼ teaspoon salt
⅛ teaspoon pepper
½ cup shredded cheese (Cheddar, Monterey Jack, or Swiss)
Paprika and dried parsley flakes, for garnish

Place butter in glass pie plate. Microwave on high 30 seconds to 1 minute. In small mixing bowl, beat together remaining ingredients except cheese. Pour into pie plate, cover loosely with waxed paper, and microwave on medium-high 4 to 5½ minutes, stirring once halfway through cooking time. Eggs should be almost firm. Sprinkle cheese evenly over top of eggs and let stand, covered, 2 to 3 minutes. Fold omelet in half, sprinkle with paprika and parsley flakes. Makes 2 servings.

Pasta-Vegetable Scramble

Makes the most of summer produce

½ cup halved thin zucchini slices
⅓ cup green onions with tops, chopped
⅓ cup red or green bell pepper, julienned
1 tablespoon butter
4 eggs
¼ cup milk
2 tablespoons Parmesan cheese, grated
1 teaspoon garlic salt
¾ teaspoon Italian seasoning
⅛ teaspoon crushed red pepper
4 ounces fettuccine or linguine, cooked and drained
6 cherry tomatoes, halved

In 10-inch omelet pan or skillet over medium heat, cook zucchini, onions, and bell pepper in butter until zucchini is crisp-tender, about 3 minutes. Meanwhile, beat together eggs, milk, cheese, and seasonings. Pour over vegetables in pan. Add pasta and tomatoes.

As egg mixture begins to set, gently draw an inverted pancake turner completely across bottom and sides of pan. Continue until eggs are thickened but still moist. (Remove scrambled eggs from pan when slightly underdone; heat retained in eggs completes the cooking.) Do not stir constantly. Serve immediately. Makes 2 servings.

Savory Scramble

Good for Sunday brunch

1 tablespoon butter or margarine
2 tablespoons chopped green or red bell pepper
2 tablespoons chopped green onions
5 large eggs
⅓ cup sour cream
¼ teaspoon pepper

¼ teaspoon salt
¼ teaspoon crumbled dried basil leaves
1 medium tomato, chopped
½ cup shredded Cheddar cheese

Combine butter, bell pepper, and onions in 1½-quart microwave-safe baking dish. Microwave on high 1 minute, until vegetables are soft. Combine eggs, sour cream, and pepper in medium mixing bowl; beat well to blend thoroughly. Fold in remaining ingredients except cheese. Pour mixture into baking dish. Cover loosely with waxed paper and microwave on medium-high 3½ to 5 minutes or until eggs are almost set, stirring every minute. Stir in cheese. Let stand, covered, 3 to 4 minutes before serving, to finish cooking eggs and melt cheese. Makes 2 to 3 servings.

Zucchini Frittata

See Back-to-Back Brunches for Twelve, p. 258.

Fondue Fromage (Cheese Fondue)

The genuine article, straight from the canton of Geneva; great for a supper party

2 loaves crusty French or Italian bread
1½ pounds unprocessed Gruyère cheese
2 teaspoons cornstarch
1 jigger (1½ ounces) kirsch brandy
1 clove garlic
¾ pint light white wine (such as Johannisberger)
Nutmeg
Pepper

Early in the day, cut bread into bite-sized pieces, each with its own crust. Set aside to get a bit stale. Grate cheese by hand or in food processor with metal blade. Set aside. Moisten cornstarch in cup with small amount of kirsch to form smooth paste. Add rest of kirsch and stir until mixture is smooth. Peel and cut garlic clove in half. Rub sides and bottom of flame-proof earthenware casserole with raw sides of garlic. Place casserole on diffuser over burner; pour in wine and heat but do not bring to boil. Gradually add grated cheese, stirring constantly. When all cheese is assimilated, add cornstarch-kirsch mixture and bring to boil for no longer than 2 minutes. Sprinkle on nutmeg and immediately place on spirit burner. Grate in pepper. Keep mixture hot. Diners spear bread cubes on long forks and swirl them around in fondue, one bite at a time. Serve with a crisp green salad and a crisp white wine. Makes 4 to 6 servings.

Sweets

Angel Food Cake with Apple-Cinnamon Glaze

A low-cholesterol treat

CAKE
1½ cups powdered sugar (sift if necessary)
1 cup cake flour
1½ cups egg whites (about 12)
1½ teaspoons cream of tartar
¼ teaspoon salt
1 cup granulated sugar
1 teaspoon vanilla extract
½ teaspoon almond extract

GLAZE
⅓ cup butter or margarine
2 cups powdered sugar
½ teaspoon ground cinnamon
2 or 3 tablespoons apple juice or cider

CAKE: Move rack to lowest position; preheat oven to 375 degrees. Mix powdered sugar and flour; reserve. Beat egg whites, cream of tartar, and salt in large bowl on high speed until stiff peaks form. Beat in granulated sugar on high, 2 tablespoons at a time; continue beating until stiff and glossy. Beat in vanilla and almond extracts on low; gently fold in flour mixture. Pour into ungreased 10 × 4-inch tube pan. Gently cut through batter with rubber spatula. Bake 30 to 40 minutes or until top crust is deep golden brown and cracks feel dry. Do not underbake. Immediately turn pan upside down onto glass bottle or metal funnel. Let hang about 2 hours or until cake is completely cool. Remove from pan. Spread top with glaze, allowing some to drizzle down side.

GLAZE: Melt butter in saucepan. Blend in powdered sugar and cinnamon. Stir in apple juice, 1 tablespoon at a time, until glaze is thin enough to drizzle.

Apple Cake with Caramel Sauce

From the Iowa Department of Agriculture

¼ cup butter or margarine
1 cup sugar
1 egg
1 cup flour
1 teaspoon baking soda
1 teaspoon ground nutmeg
½ teaspoon ground cinnamon
2 cups diced apples
½ cup chopped nuts
Caramel Sauce (see following recipe)

Preheat oven to 350 degrees. In small mixing bowl, cream butter and sugar until fluffy. Add egg. Beat well. In small bowl, combine flour, baking soda, nutmeg, and cinnamon. Add to creamed mixture. Beat just until combined. By hand, fold in apples and nuts. Spread batter in greased 8-inch square baking pan. Bake 35 to 45 minutes or until done. Serve warm with Caramel Sauce. Makes 9 servings.

Caramel Sauce

½ cup butter or margarine
½ cup packed brown sugar
½ cup sugar
½ cup heavy cream
1 tablespoon vanilla extract

In small saucepan, melt butter. Stir in sugars and cream. Bring just to boiling over medium heat, stirring constantly. Remove from heat and stir in vanilla. Serve over warm cake. Makes 1½ cups sauce.

Chocolate Rum Cake

CAKE
1 (18½-ounce) package chocolate cake mix
1 (3¾-ounce) package chocolate instant pudding and pie filling
4 eggs
1 cup rum, divided
¾ cup water
½ cup oil
1 (12-ounce) package (2 cups) semisweet chocolate chips, divided

GLAZE
1 (10- to 12-ounce) jar (1 cup) raspberry preserves
Remaining ½ cup rum

FROSTING
Remaining 1 cup chocolate morsels
2 tablespoons shortening

DRIZZLE
1 (1-ounce) square vanilla baking bar
1 teaspoon water

CAKE: Preheat oven to 350 degrees. Combine cake mix, pudding, eggs, ½ cup rum, water, and oil in large mixing bowl. Beat at low speed until moistened. Beat at medium speed 2 minutes. Stir in chocolate chips. Pour batter into greased and floured 12-cup Bundt pan or 10-inch tube pan. Bake 50 to 60 minutes until cake tests done. Cool in pan 15 minutes. Remove from pan and cool on rack.

GLAZE: In small saucepan, heat raspberry preserves and remaining ½ cup rum. Strain through sieve to remove seeds. Place cake on serving plate. Prick surface of cake with fork. Brush raspberry glaze evenly over cake, allowing cake to absorb glaze. Repeat until all glaze has been absorbed.

FROSTING: In bowl, combine remaining 1 cup chocolate chips and shortening. Microwave on high 1 minute or until melted. Stir until smooth. Or heat mixture over hot (not boiling) water until chocolate melts and mixture is smooth. Spoon chocolate icing over cake. Let stand 10 minutes.

DRIZZLE: In small bowl, combine vanilla baking bar and water. Microwave on high 30 seconds or until melted. Or melt over hot (not boiling) water. Drizzle on top of chocolate icing.

Jean Tallman, food editor of the late *Des Moines Tribune,* says a former managing editor of the *Register and Tribune,* Frank Eyerly, agreed with a reader who wrote, "If your children become alcoholic, you need only to look to your kitchen for the reason why."

"Knowing that the newspaper accepted no liquor ads, Frank decided I was using entirely too much alcohol in recipes. So I changed half a cup of rum to half a cup of rum flavoring for one recipe. Needless to say, a reader called, complaining that her rum flavoring bottle contained only 1½ ounces and how many did she really have to buy!"

Cocoa Cappuccino Cake

Two classic flavors in an easy cake

1 cup slivered almonds, divided
¾ cup shortening
1¾ cups sugar
3 eggs
1 teaspoon vanilla extract
¼ teaspoon almond extract
2 cups flour
¾ cup unsweetened cocoa powder
4 teaspoons instant coffee crystals
1 teaspoon baking soda
½ teaspoon baking powder
½ teaspoon salt
1¼ cups milk
Cocoa Cappuccino Icing (see recipe, p. 200)

Spread almonds in single layer on baking sheet. Place in cold oven; turn oven to 350 degrees and bake 9 to 11 minutes, stirring occasionally, until golden brown. Cool. Cream shortening with sugar, eggs, and extracts until fluffy. Combine flour with cocoa powder, coffee crystals, baking soda, baking powder, and salt; mix well. Blend dry ingredients into creamed mixture alternately with milk. Stir in ½ cup toasted almonds. Pour into greased and floured 13 × 9-inch baking pan. Bake 40 to 45 minutes or until pick inserted in center comes out clean. Cool on wire rack. Frost with Cocoa Cappuccino Icing and sprinkle with remaining ½ cup toasted almonds. Makes 16 servings.

Golden Rum Cake

CAKE
1 cup chopped pecans or walnuts
1 (18½-ounce) package yellow cake mix
1 (3¼-ounce) package vanilla instant pudding and pie filling

4 eggs
½ cup cold water
½ cup vegetable oil
½ cup dark rum

GLAZE
½ pound butter or margarine
¼ cup water
1 cup sugar
½ cup dark rum

CAKE: Preheat oven to 325 degrees. Grease and flour 10-inch tube pan or 12-cup Bundt pan. Sprinkle nuts over bottom of pan. Mix remaining cake ingredients together and blend. Pour batter over nuts. Bake 1 hour. Cool. Invert on serving plate. Prick top with fork.

GLAZE: Melt butter in saucepan. Stir in water and sugar. Boil 5 minutes, stirring constantly. Remove from heat. Stir in rum. Spoon and brush glaze evenly over top and sides of cake. Allow cake to absorb glaze. Repeat until all glaze is used.

Heavenly Chocolate Rolls

CAKE
3 tablespoons unsweetened cocoa powder
1 package angel food cake mix

FILLING
½ ounce grated semisweet chocolate
1 (8-ounce) container frozen whipped topping, thawed

DRIZZLE
⅓ cup semisweet chocolate chips
2 teaspoons shortening
Powdered sugar

CAKE: Preheat oven to 350 degrees. Line 2 15 × 10-inch jelly roll pans with foil. Add cocoa powder to cake flour and prepare cake according to package directions. Divide batter between foil-lined pans. Spread evenly. Cut through batter with knife or spatula to remove large air bubbles. Bake 15 minutes or until set. Invert cakes immediately onto lint-free dish towels dusted with powdered sugar. Remove foil carefully. Roll each cake up in towel jelly-roll fashion. Cool.

FILLING: Fold grated chocolate into whipped topping. Unroll cakes. Spread half of filling over each cake to edges. Reroll and place cakes seam-side down on serving plate.

DRIZZLE: Combine chocolate chips and shortening in zip-top plastic bag. Place bag in hot water for several minutes. Dry with toweling. Knead until blended and chocolate is smooth. Snip pinpoint corner in bag. Drizzle over rolls. Refrigerate until ready to serve. Dust cake rolls with powdered sugar. Makes 12 servings.

Irish Whiskey Cake

See Tea Party for Twelve, p. 253.

Mini Marble Pound Cakes

1 (6-ounce) package semisweet chocolate chips
½ cup milk, divided
2½ cups flour
1½ teaspoons baking powder
½ teaspoon salt
1¼ cups butter, softened
2 cups sugar
5 eggs
1 tablespoon vanilla extract

Preheat oven to 325 degrees. Place chocolate chips and ¼ cup milk in small microwave-safe bowl. Microwave on high 1 to 2 minutes or until chocolate melts; stir after 1 minute. Set aside to cool. Or heat in small saucepan over low heat 2 to 3 minutes until chocolate melts. Combine flour, baking powder, and salt; set aside. Cream butter and sugar in large mixing bowl until light and fluffy. Add eggs and vanilla; mix well.

Add flour mixture; mix until blended. Transfer 3⅓ cups batter to medium bowl; stir in remaining ¼ cup milk and set aside. Pour reserved chocolate mixture into remaining batter in mixing bowl; blend well. In each of 4 well-buttered 5¾ × 3¼ × 2-inch loaf pans (foil pans can be used), alternately pour white and chocolate layers of batter. Once all batter has been used, gently swirl batters with table knife.

Place loaf pans on cookie sheet. Bake about 1 hour to 1 hour 10 minutes or until wooden pick inserted in center comes out clean. Cool in pans on wire racks 10 minutes. Remove from pans. Transfer to wire racks; cool completely. Makes 4 small loaves.

Orange Spice Cake

A reader favorite

CAKE
¾ cup salad dressing (such as Miracle Whip)
1 (18½-ounce) package yellow cake mix
1 envelope whipped topping mix
¾ cup orange juice
3 eggs
½ teaspoon ground cinnamon
¼ teaspoon ground cloves
¼ teaspoon ground nutmeg
1 cup finely chopped walnuts (optional)

GLAZE
1½ cups powdered sugar
2 tablespoons milk
1 teaspoon grated orange peel

CAKE: Preheat oven to 350 degrees. Mix together all cake ingredients except nuts at medium speed 2 minutes. Stir in nuts, if desired. Pour into greased and floured 10-inch fluted tube pan. Bake 35 to 40 minutes or until wooden pick inserted in center comes out clean. Let stand 10 minutes; remove from pan. Cool.

GLAZE: Blend powdered sugar and milk until smooth. Add orange peel. Drizzle over cake. Makes 12 servings.

Peanut Butter Banana Cake

CAKE
1 cup mashed ripe bananas
½ cup butter or margarine, softened
½ cup creamy peanut butter
1 cup whipping cream
3 eggs
1 package pudding-included butter-flavor cake mix
2 tablespoons flour

FROSTING
1 can ready-to-spread vanilla frosting
½ teaspoon banana extract or vanilla extract
3 to 4 drops yellow food coloring (optional)

GLAZE
½ cup powdered sugar
2 tablespoons creamy peanut butter
2 tablespoons milk
½ teaspoon vanilla extract

GARNISH
2 medium bananas, thinly sliced

CAKE: Preheat oven to 350 degrees. Generously grease and flour 13 × 9-inch pan. In large bowl, combine mashed bananas and butter; mix well (mixture will look slightly curdled). Add peanut butter; beat well. Add whipping cream and eggs; beat at high speed until smooth. Add cake mix and flour; beat at low speed until moistened; then beat 2 minutes at high speed. Pour into prepared pan. Bake 45 to 55 minutes or until pick inserted in center comes out clean. Cool 15 minutes; remove from pan, if desired. Cool completely.

FROSTING: In small bowl, combine frosting ingredients; stir until smooth and creamy. Frost cake.

GLAZE: In small bowl, combine glaze ingredients; beat until smooth. Drizzle glaze over frosting. Just before serving, garnish with banana slices. Store in refrigerator. Makes 12 to 15 servings.

Pineanna Nut Cake

An old recipe for Hummingbird Cake

3⅓ cups cake flour
2 cups sugar
1 teaspoon baking soda
1 teaspoon salt
1 teaspoon ground cinnamon
1 cup vegetable oil
3 eggs, slightly beaten
2 cups chopped ripe bananas (about 4 medium)
1 cup chopped pecans
1½ teaspoons vanilla extract
1 (8-ounce) can crushed pineapple in juice, undrained
Cream Cheese Frosting (see recipe, p. 201)
½ cup chopped pecans for garnish (optional)

Preheat oven to 350 degrees. Grease and flour 3 (9-inch) round pans. In large bowl, mix flour, sugar, baking soda, salt, and cinnamon. Add oil and eggs. Stir until all dry ingredients are moistened; do not beat. Stir in bananas, pecans, vanilla, and pineapple. Divide batter evenly among pans. Bake 25 to 30 minutes or until pick inserted in center comes out clean. Cool 10 minutes; remove from pans. Cool completely on wire racks.

With Cream Cheese Frosting, frost tops of layers and stack; frost side and top of cake. Sprinkle pecans on top, if desired. Cut cake with sharp knife; refrigerate any remaining cake. Makes 1 triple-layer cake.

Quickie Cupcakes

From Jennifer Phelps of Carlisle, Iowa

½ cup boiling water
1 ounce unsweetened baking chocolate
¼ cup butter
1 cup flour

1 cup sugar
¾ teaspoon baking soda
¼ teaspoon salt
¼ cup buttermilk
1 egg, beaten
1 teaspoon vanilla extract
Espresso Frosting (see recipe, p. 201)

Preheat oven to 375 degrees. Combine water, chocolate, and butter; stir until blended and chocolate and butter are melted. Sift together flour, sugar, baking soda, and salt. Add to chocolate mixture. Combine buttermilk, egg, and vanilla. Add to chocolate mixture and blend well. Line muffin cups with paper baking cups. Pour in batter until cups are ⅔ full. Bake 25 minutes. Frost with Espresso Frosting. Makes 12 cupcakes.

Buttercream Frosting

A basic you'll use over and over

3 cups powdered sugar
½ cup butter, softened
⅓ cup milk or half-and-half cream
1 teaspoon vanilla extract
Food coloring (optional)

Cream sugar and butter in large mixing bowl until light and fluffy. Add milk and vanilla; beat until smooth. Add additional milk, if necessary, to reach desired consistency for spreading. Stir in food coloring, if desired.

Cocoa Cappuccino Icing

¼ cup butter
¼ cup unsweetened cocoa powder
1 teaspoon instant coffee crystals
2 tablespoons light corn syrup

2 tablespoons milk
2 cups powdered sugar, sifted
1 teaspoon vanilla extract
¼ teaspoon almond extract

Melt butter in small saucepan. Blend in cocoa powder and coffee crystals to dissolve. Stir in corn syrup, milk, powdered sugar, and extracts; beat until smooth. Spread over cooled cake.

Cream Cheese Frosting

1 (8-ounce) package cream cheese, softened
½ cup butter or margarine, softened
1 (1-pound) package powdered sugar (about 3½ cups)
1 teaspoon vanilla extract

Beat cream cheese and butter in large bowl on medium speed until smooth. Beat in powdered sugar and vanilla until light and fluffy.

Espresso Frosting

From Jennifer Phelps of Carlisle, Iowa

½ cup butter
⅓ cup unsweetened cocoa powder
1 to 1½ cups powdered sugar, sifted
½ cup espresso or strong coffee

Cream butter until soft. Add cocoa and powdered sugar; stir in coffee until frosting is thick spreading consistency. Frost cooled cupcakes generously, using fork to swirl frosting into peaks.

Double Chocolate Cheesecake

See Champagne Brunch for Twenty-four, p. 237.

Light Strawberry Cheesecake

CRUST
1½ cups Graham cracker crumbs
3 tablespoons melted butter or margarine

FILLING
1 (15-ounce) carton part-skim ricotta cheese
1 cup sugar, divided
⅔ cup flour
4 eggs, separated
2 tablespoons grated lemon peel
2 teaspoons vanilla extract
1 cup nonfat sour cream substitute

SAUCE
3 pints stemmed strawberries, divided
Remaining ¼ cup sugar
4 teaspoons lemon juice

GLAZE
¼ cup red currant jelly, melted

CRUST: Preheat oven to 300 degrees. In medium bowl, mix crumbs and butter. Press onto bottom and 2 inches up sides of lightly greased 9-inch springform pan; set aside.

FILLING: In mixing bowl, beat cheese until smooth. Add ¾ cup of sugar, flour, egg yolks, lemon peel, and vanilla; mix well. Thoroughly blend in sour cream substitute. In another bowl, beat egg whites until stiff but not dry; fold into cheese mixture. Pour into prepared crust; smooth top. Bake 1 hour. Turn off oven; cool in oven 1 hour with door ajar. Remove from oven; chill thoroughly.

SAUCE: In blender or food processor, puree 2 pints of strawberries with remaining ¼ cup sugar and lemon juice; strain sauce to remove seeds. Cover and chill.

Halve remaining strawberries and arrange on top of cake. Brush berries with currant jelly. Cut cake into wedges; serve with sauce. Makes 14 servings.

CINNAMON ORNAMENTS

Even though it's not for anything edible, this likely is the most requested recipe ever published in *The Des Moines Register*. The reason? Aromatic cinnamon ornaments became popular as tree or window trims during the holidays a few years ago. There were times when we mailed out at least ten copies a day of directions for making them. The how-to recipe is from Tone's Spices of Des Moines.

1 cup ground cinnamon
1 teaspoon ground allspice
1 teaspoon ground cloves
1 teaspoon ground nutmeg
1 cup applesauce

Mix together all dry ingredients. Add applesauce a little at a time. (Mixture should have the consistency of Play-Doh, so you can work it with your hands.) If mixture is too dry, add 1 to 2 tablespoons more applesauce. Roll dough out to ¼-inch thickness on ungreased surface. If mixture is too sticky to handle, sprinkle working surface and mixture with ground cinnamon. Use sharp-edged cookie cutters to cut out desired shapes. Place on level surface to dry. Air-dry 4 to 5 days. Recipe makes about 24 ornaments, depending on size of cookie cutters.

NOTE: A fine wire from a craft shop can be cut in short pieces, bent into an inverted "U" shape, and inserted at the top of each ornament before drying to serve as a hanger for yarn or ribbon. Ornaments lighten in color as they dry. Wrap carefully in plastic wrap and store in cool, dry place to save from year to year.

Pumpkin Cheesecake

See Holiday Dinner, p. 269.

Basic Butter Cookies

Good for a baking marathon

2 cups butter
1½ cups sugar
2 eggs
1 teaspoon vanilla extract
5 cups flour
2 teaspoons baking powder
¼ teaspoon salt

Cream butter in large mixing bowl. Gradually add sugar and beat until light and fluffy. Blend in eggs and vanilla. Combine flour, baking powder, and salt. Gradually add to creamed mixture; mix well. Divide dough into four equal portions. Mix and shape dough for each variety.

CUTOUTS: Preheat oven to 375 degrees. Roll a fourth of dough on lightly floured surface to ⅛-inch thickness. Cut into desired shapes with floured cookie cutters. Place on ungreased cookie sheets. Bake 6 to 8 minutes. Cool completely on wire racks; decorate as desired. Makes about 24 cookies.

PEPPERMINT BALLS: Preheat oven to 375 degrees. Beat ¼ cup crushed peppermint candy and ¼ teaspoon peppermint extract into a fourth of dough. Shape into 1-inch balls. Place on ungreased cookie sheets. Sprinkle with red colored sugar. Bake 8 to 10 minutes. Cool completely on wire racks. Makes about 24 cookies.

SPICY FRUIT BALLS: Preheat oven to 375 degrees. Beat ½ teaspoon cinnamon, ½ cup currants, and ½ cup chopped, mixed candied fruit into a fourth of dough. Shape into 1-inch balls. Place on ungreased cookie sheets. Bake 8 to 10 minutes. While still warm, roll in confectioner's sugar. Cool completely on wire racks. Makes about 24 cookies.

CHOCOLATE SLICES: Beat 1 ounce (1 square) melted unsweetened chocolate into a fourth of dough. Shape into log about 1½ inches in diameter. Roll in chopped nuts. Wrap in plastic wrap and refrigerate several hours or overnight. Preheat oven to 375 degrees. Cut dough into ⅛-inch-thick slices. Place on ungreased cookie sheets. Bake 6 to 8 minutes. Cool completely on wire racks. Makes about 36 cookies.

Holidays mean special foods in Iowa. There's ham or lamb for Easter Sunday, honey cake for Rosh Hashanah, turkey 'n' trimmings for Thanksgiving, hot dogs or brats, burgers, and ice cream for Fourth of July. But Christmas? Some people prefer ham, turkey, crown roast, or goose. There's just no standard. Each family has its traditions.

But I've decided the quintessential Christmas food is cookies. Everyone bakes them, everyone gives them, everyone eats them, everyone loves them. I get calls every year from readers who want to know when our cookie page will run.

Mom's Sugar Cookies

From Clara Marlow of Perry, Iowa

3 cups flour
2 teaspoons baking powder
1 teaspoon baking soda
¼ teaspoon ground nutmeg
1 cup shortening
2 eggs
1 cup sugar
4 tablespoons milk
1 teaspoon vanilla extract

Preheat oven to 400 degrees. Sift together flour, baking powder, baking soda, and nutmeg. Cut in shortening. Add eggs, sugar, milk, and vanilla. Beat thoroughly. Roll out dough and cut with cookie cutters. Bake until lightly browned. Frost, if desired. Amount varies, depending on size of cookie cutters.

Summer Sugar Cookies

From Colleen Beattie of Doe Run Inn, Runnells, Iowa

1 cup oil
1 cup margarine
1 cup powdered sugar
1 cup granulated sugar
2 eggs
5 cups flour
1 teaspoon cream of tartar
1 teaspoon baking soda
1 teaspoon vanilla or almond extract
Sugar for dipping

Preheat oven to 350 degrees. Mix first five ingredients. Blend in remaining ingredients except sugar for dipping. Roll dough into balls and dip in sugar. Place on ungreased cookie sheet. Press tops with tumbler that has been dipped in sugar. Bake 8 minutes. Makes about 60 cookies.

Grandma's Chocolate Drop Cookies

From Evelyn DeLanoit of Fort Dodge, Iowa

1½ cups flour
¼ teaspoon salt
1 teaspoon baking powder
2 squares unsweetened baking chocolate
½ cup shortening, melted
1 cup brown sugar
1 egg, slightly beaten
½ cup milk
1 teaspoon vanilla extract
Frosting, if desired

Preheat oven to 375 degrees. Sift together flour, salt, and baking powder. Set aside. Melt chocolate and add to melted shortening. Add sugar, egg, milk, and vanilla to chocolate and shortening mixture. Add sifted ingredients and let stand 10 minutes. Drop from teaspoon onto greased cookie sheet. Bake 12 to 15 minutes. Frost, if desired, with Buttercream Frosting, Espresso Frosting (see recipes), or your favorite chocolate icing. Makes 36 cookies.

Rolled Chocolate Chip Cookies

From Kate Lee of St. Louis

1 cup shortening
1 cup brown sugar
1 cup granulated sugar
2 eggs
1 teaspoon vanilla extract
1½ cups flour
1 teaspoon baking soda
1 teaspoon salt
3 cups quick rolled oats
10 to 12 ounces semisweet chocolate chips

Preheat oven to 350 degrees. Blend shortening, sugars, and eggs. Add vanilla and stir to blend. In separate bowl, mix flour, soda, and salt. Add to shortening-sugar mixture. Stir in oats and chocolate chips. Shape into roll about size of rolling pin and cover with waxed paper. Refrigerate dough overnight. Cut into ½-inch slices and place on ungreased cookie sheet. Bake 10 to 12 minutes. Makes about 24 cookies.

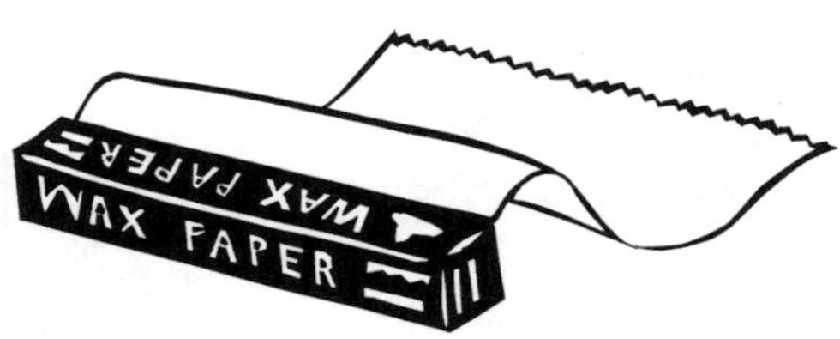

As with most facets of publishing, the best part always is the people you meet, people you might never encounter any other way. Some years ago a woman called. She and her sister remembered a dessert from their childhood—madeleines, a sponge cake-like dessert made famous by Marcel Proust in *Remembrance of Things Past.* Depressions in the little cakes are usually filled with fruits, jams, or puddings. Madeleines require special cake pans, something like those for cupcakes.

You know how it is. They were on a mission to find a madeleine pan and became relentless in their pursuit. They couldn't find one anywhere. I said I would save their names, and if I ever ran across such a baking pan, I'd send them the information.

Some months later, there they were in a cooking catalog—madeleine pans. I called the sisters, and they were thrilled. They ordered the pan and began experimenting.

Then one day came the call. "Would you please come to a tea party? Of course, we're serving madeleines."

What could I say? I visited the sisters in their home, decorated with fabrics and furnishings from another era. They were ecstatic to find a piece of their past and to share it. It just shows how comforting food really can be.

Chocolate Peanut Butter Thumbprints

1½ cups flour
⅓ cup unsweetened cocoa powder
1½ teaspoons baking powder
¼ teaspoon salt
1 (12-ounce) package (2 cups) semisweet chocolate chips, divided
1 cup sugar
About 1 cup chunky or creamy peanut butter, divided
⅓ cup butter or margarine, softened
1½ teaspoons vanilla extract
2 eggs

Preheat oven to 350 degrees. In small bowl, combine flour, cocoa powder, baking powder, and salt. In small heavy saucepan over low heat, melt 1 cup chocolate chips; stir until smooth. In large mixing bowl, cream sugar, ⅓ cup peanut butter, butter, and vanilla. Beat in melted chocolate. Add eggs, one at a time, beating well after each addition. Gradually beat in dry ingredients. Stir in remaining 1 cup chocolate chips. Cover; chill just until firm. Shape into 1½-inch balls; press thumb into tops to make about ½-inch-deep depressions. Place on ungreased cookie sheets. Fill each depression with about ½ teaspoon peanut butter. Bake 10 to 15 minutes or until sides are set but centers are still slightly soft. Cool 2 minutes. Remove to wire racks to cool completely. Makes about 42 cookies.

Coconut Macaroons

From Robin Tarbell-Thomas of Centerville, Iowa

½ cup egg whites
¼ teaspoon salt
1¼ cups sugar
½ teaspoon vanilla extract
2½ cups shredded coconut

Preheat oven to 325 degrees. With electric mixer, beat egg whites and salt until soft peaks form; gradually add sugar, beating until stiff peaks form. Fold in vanilla and coconut. Drop from teaspoon onto cookie sheets covered with parchment paper. Bake 20 minutes. Cool slightly before removing from cookie sheets. Makes 24 to 30 cookies.

Cookies on a Stick

They look like caramel apples

COOKIES
1 cup sugar
½ cup butter or margarine, softened
½ cup shortening
1½ teaspoons vanilla extract
2 eggs
3 cups flour
½ teaspoon baking soda
½ teaspoon salt
Red paste food color (optional)

GLAZE
1 (14-ounce) package vanilla caramels
¼ cup water

COOKIES: Preheat oven to 400 degrees. Cream together sugar, butter, and shortening in large bowl. Stir in vanilla and eggs. Stir in flour, baking soda, and salt. Tint with food color, if desired. Roll dough ¼ inch thick on lightly floured, cloth-covered surface. Cut with 3-inch round or apple-shaped cookie cutter. Place on ungreased cookie sheets. Insert wooden stick horizontally into edge of each cookie. Bake 8 to 9 minutes or until edges are light brown. Cool about 2 minutes before removing from cookie sheets. Cool completely on wire rack.

GLAZE: Heat caramels and water over low heat, stirring frequently, until melted and smooth. If glaze becomes too stiff, reheat over low heat, stirring constantly, until softened. Spread top third of each cookie (opposite wooden stick) with glaze. Hold cookie upright to allow glaze to drizzle down cookie. Makes about 24 cookies.

Nutty Aunt Lissy's Nana Cookies

From Jennifer Phelps of Carlisle, Iowa

1 cup sugar
½ cup butter
2 medium eggs
½ teaspoon vanilla extract
½ teaspoon lemon extract
¼ cup mashed banana
1½ cups rolled oats
2 cups sifted flour
¾ teaspoon baking soda
1 teaspoon baking powder
1½ teaspoons salt
½ cup chopped hickory nuts or English walnuts

Preheat oven to 350 degrees. Cream sugar and butter; add eggs and blend in flavorings, mashed banana, and rolled oats. Combine dry ingredients and sift into batter. Fold in nuts. Drop with teaspoon 2 inches apart on well-greased cookie sheets. Bake 12 to 15 minutes. Makes about 48 cookies.

Apple Pie Bars

FILLING
1 cup sugar
1 teaspoon cinnamon
3 teaspoons grated lemon peel, divided
8 cups peeled, sliced apples
½ cup golden raisins

CRUST
2½ cups flour
1 tablespoon sugar
1 teaspoon salt
1 cup shortening

1 egg yolk
Milk
1 egg white, lightly beaten

DRIZZLE
1 cup sifted powdered sugar
2 tablespoons lemon juice

FILLING: Preheat oven to 375 degrees. In extra-large bowl, combine sugar, cinnamon, and 1 teaspoon lemon peel. Add apple slices, tossing to coat. Stir in raisins. Set aside.

CRUST: In a large bowl, stir together flour, sugar, remaining 2 teaspoons lemon peel, and salt. Cut in shortening until pieces are size of small peas. In 1 cup measure, place egg yolk. Add enough milk to measure ½ cup. Add to flour mixture, mixing just until moistened. Divide dough in half. On floured surface, roll half of pastry into 17 × 12-inch rectangle. Ease pastry into 15½ × 10½-inch jelly roll pan. There should be overhang of pastry. Arrange apple slices evenly over pastry in pan. Roll out remaining dough into 15½ × 10½-inch rectangle. Fit dough over apples. Seal and crimp pastry edges together. Cut several slits in top pastry and brush with beaten egg white. Bake 45 to 50 minutes or until crust is golden.

DRIZZLE: In small bowl, combine powdered sugar and lemon juice until smooth. Drizzle over warm pastry. Makes 12 to 16 servings.

Fourth of July Bars

Adds a touch of red, white, and blue

CRUST
1 cup quick or old-fashioned rolled oats
¾ cup flour
⅓ cup firmly packed brown sugar
¼ teaspoon baking soda
⅓ cup margarine, melted

FILLING
2 (8-ounce) packages cream cheese, softened
¾ cup granulated sugar

2 tablespoons flour
1 teaspoon vanilla extract
2 eggs

TOPPING
2 cups blueberries, raspberries, or sliced strawberries
½ cup strawberry preserves

CRUST: Preheat oven to 350 degrees. Grease 13 × 9-inch baking pan. Mix together rolled oats, flour, brown sugar, and baking soda. Add margarine, mixing until crumbly. Press crust mixture into bottom of greased pan; bake 10 minutes.

FILLING: Beat cream cheese, sugar, flour, and vanilla until creamy. Add eggs, one at a time, beating well after each egg. Pour over baked crust. Bake 25 minutes. Cool; chill. Store covered in refrigerator.

TOPPING: Combine berries and preserves and cover top of bars. Makes about 24 bars.

One thing you learn early on in the food business is that you can't please everyone all the time. Some like plain and simple; some prefer elegant and fancy. One fall day in 1994 we had published a variation on a classic thumbprint cookie. This one was an oatmeal cookie, topped with a candy kiss. Shortly thereafter I was reading a thank-you note from a reader in Eldora for publishing that recipe: "I'm sure it will become a family favorite for special occasions. We just loved it."

Then the telephone rang. A Des Moines–area woman wanted to know if there was something wrong with the same recipe. Her husband thought it was bland, with little flavor. She wasn't amused when I laughed out loud, until I read her the note in my hand. She laughed, too, and decided to make the cookies again. But next time she was going to feed the candy kisses to her husband and save the cookies for herself.

Rice Chex Bars

From Dan Viall of Des Moines, Iowa

1 cup sugar
1 cup light corn syrup
1 cup chunky peanut butter
1 teaspoon vanilla extract
1 cup peanuts
6 cups Rice Chex cereal

Boil sugar and syrup in large pan 30 seconds. Stir in peanut butter and vanilla. Fold in peanuts and cereal. Pour into greased 13 × 9-inch pan or drop by spoonfuls onto waxed paper. Makes about 24 squares.

VARIATIONS
Use Special K cereal instead of Rice Chex.
Use about 12 cups of popped popcorn instead of cereal; omit peanuts.

Apple Streusel Treat

Easy-to-fix dessert

STREUSEL
1 cup baking mix (such as Bisquick)
½ cup chopped nuts
⅓ cup brown sugar
3 tablespoons firm butter or margarine

FILLING
6 cups thinly sliced, peeled tart apples
1¼ teaspoons ground cinnamon
¼ teaspoon ground nutmeg
¼ cup milk
2 tablespoons butter or margarine, softened
2 eggs
1 cup sugar
¾ cup baking mix (such as Bisquick)

STREUSEL: Preheat oven to 350 degrees. Grease 13 × 9-inch baking dish. Mix streusel ingredients; set aside.

FILLING: Spread apples in baking dish. Blend remaining filling ingredients 15 seconds in blender on high or 1 minute with hand mixer or until smooth. Pour over apples. Sprinkle with streusel. Bake about 55 minutes or until knife inserted in center comes out clean; cool. Makes 12 to 15 servings.

Pie Crust

For 8- or 9-inch double-crust pie

2¼ cups flour
½ teaspoon salt
11 tablespoons chilled butter or lard, cut into small pieces
7 tablespoons chilled vegetable shortening
4 to 5 tablespoons ice water

Mix flour and salt. Cut in butter with pastry blender. Add shortening, cutting in with pastry blender until dough looks like coarse cornmeal. Add water a tablespoon at a time, folding dough over to mix. Add just enough water to make dough hold together. Divide into 2 balls, flatten into thick disks, cover with plastic wrap, and refrigerate 30 minutes. Remove from refrigerator, unwrap, dust lightly with flour, and roll out into ⅛-inch-thick crusts.

Country Apple Pie

1 tablespoon lemon juice
5 tablespoons butter or margarine, divided
1¼ cups sugar, divided
1½ teaspoons ground allspice, divided
1 teaspoon cinnamon
½ cup plus 2 tablespoons flour, divided
All-purpose flour (unsifted)
6 cups peeled, sliced tart apples (about 1½ pounds)
9-inch unbaked pie shell

Preheat oven to 375 degrees. In a small saucepan, combine lemon juice and 1 tablespoon butter. Heat until butter melts. Set aside. In large bowl, combine ¾ cup sugar, 1 teaspoon allspice, cinnamon, and 2 tablespoons flour. Add apples; toss to coat. Add butter and lemon juice mixture; toss to coat. Turn into pie shell. In small bowl, combine remaining ½ cup flour, ½ cup sugar, and ½ teaspoon allspice. Add remaining 4 tablespoons butter; cut into small pieces using pastry blender or two knives used scissor-fashion until mixture resembles coarse crumbs. Sprinkle over apples. Bake until apples are tender, 45 to 50 minutes. Cool on wire rack. Serve warm. Makes 1 pie.

Food is the "prize" of choice in many Iowa activities. Charity auctions offer gourmet dinners or specialty foods to top bidders. Prizes include such things as bread made by Father Michael Hess, president of Dowling High School of West Des Moines. Southeast of Des Moines, between Carlisle and Indianola in Palmyra Township, Armetta Keeney, a perennial pie winner at the Iowa State Fair, helps the attendance at her country church. Every Father's Day, she bakes pecan pies for all the dads in the congregation. Once she observed a father sitting outside in his car during the service. Yes, he got in line at the appropriate time to collect his pie.

Chocolate Maple Pecan Pie

From the French Room, Adolphus Hotel, Dallas

1½ cups maple syrup
6 eggs
¾ cup sugar
⅓ cup butter, melted
3 ounces bitter chocolate, melted
2 cups chopped pecans
9-inch unbaked pie shell

Preheat oven to 350 degrees. Combine syrup, eggs, sugar, butter, and chocolate in medium mixing bowl. Mix until smooth. Sprinkle in pecans. Pour into pie shell and bake 30 to 40 minutes. Center of pie should be firm to touch. Cool before serving. Makes 1 pie.

Lemon Pie

From Armetta Keeney of Carlisle, Iowa

2 cups sugar
4 egg yolks
2 cups water
½ cup cornstarch
Dash of salt
2 tablespoons butter
8 tablespoons freshly squeezed lemon juice
9-inch baked pie shell
No-Weep Meringue (see following recipe)

In saucepan, blend sugar, egg yolks, water, cornstarch, and salt. Cook until thickened and cornstarch is cooked. Remove from heat and add butter and lemon juice. Pour in baked shell and top with meringue. Makes 1 pie.

No-Weep Meringue

From Armetta Keeney of Carlisle, Iowa

1 tablespoon sugar
1 tablespoon cornstarch
½ cup water
3 or 4 egg whites
1 tablespoon sugar per egg white

Preheat oven to 350 degrees. Put sugar, cornstarch, and water in saucepan. Cook mixture until thick and clear, stirring constantly; set aside. In stainless steel or glass bowl, beat 3 or 4 egg whites until frothy, adding 1 tablespoon sugar per egg white. Continue beating until very stiff. Remove beater and add cooked mixture. Mix in gently by hand (do not beat with mixer or meringue will get tough). Spread meringue on filling and bake 12 to 15 minutes or until meringue is browned. Makes enough meringue for 1 pie.

Key Lime Pie

PIE
6 egg yolks, beaten
1 (14-ounce) can sweetened condensed milk
½ cup Key lime juice
9-inch unbaked pie shell

MERINGUE
6 egg whites, stiffly beaten
4 tablespoons sugar

PIE: Preheat oven to 350 degrees. Combine egg yolks and milk. Add and blend in Key lime juice and put in pie shell.

MERINGUE: Combine egg whites and sugar. Spread on Key lime filling, making attractive swirls or peaks. Bake about 12 to 15 minutes. Makes 1 pie.

Rhubarb Pie

From Judy Arnold of Indianola, Iowa

CRUST
2 cups flour
1 teaspoon salt
⅔ cup shortening
5 to 7 tablespoons cold water

FILLING
1 tablespoon crushed ginger root
3 tablespoons orange juice concentrate, thawed
1⅔ cups sugar
⅓ cup flour
4 cups rhubarb
1 tablespoon butter

CRUST: Preheat oven to 450 degrees. Combine flour and salt; mix well. With pastry blender, cut in shortening and mix until uniform. Sprinkle cold water into mixture, 1 tablespoon at a time until dough is moistened. Divide dough in half; shape into two balls. On floured surface, roll first ball of dough into circle 1 inch larger than inverted pie pan. Carefully lift and place in pan.

FILLING: Simmer ginger root in orange juice 5 minutes. Mix sugar and flour. Cut rhubarb into small pieces and add to sugar and flour. Strain ginger root from orange juice and add to rhubarb mixture; mix well. Place rhubarb mixture in unbaked pie crust. Dot filling with butter.

TOP CRUST: Roll second ball of dough into circle and place over filling. Seal edges and flute. Make slits in top of crust to allow steam to escape. Bake 10 minutes. Reduce heat to 350 degrees and bake an additional 45 minutes. Makes 1 pie.

Lemon Tart Miniatures

See Tea Party for Twelve, p. 251.

Pecan Tart Miniatures

See Tea Party for Twelve, p. 251.

Southern Exposure Peach Pie

From Vicky Smith of Lamoni, Iowa

CRUST
2 cups flour
1 teaspoon salt
¾ cup shortening
9 tablespoons water

FILLING
5 cups fresh peaches, peeled and sliced
¼ teaspoon salt
2 tablespoons cornstarch
1¼ cups sugar
2 tablespoons butter
Dash of cinnamon

CRUST: Preheat oven to 350 degrees. Combine flour and salt in medium bowl. Cut in shortening using pastry blender (or two knives) until flour is blended to form pea-sized chunks. Sprinkle with water, 1 tablespoon at a time. Toss lightly with fork until dough will form ball. Divide dough in half. On floured surface, roll each half separately. Transfer bottom crust to 8- or 9-inch pie plate. Trim edges. Moisten pastry edge with water.

FILLING: Mix filling ingredients and put into unbaked pie shell. Lift top crust onto filled pie. Trim ½ inch beyond edge of pie plate. Fold top edge under bottom crust. Flute. Cut slits or designs in top crust to allow steam to escape. Bake 1 hour. Makes 1 pie.

Tart Crust

See Tea Party for Twelve, p. 252.

Rhubarb Dessert

From Ruth Jones of Shawnee, Kansas

CRUST
1 cup flour
5 tablespoons powdered sugar
½ cup butter or margarine

FILLING
3 eggs, beaten
1¼ cups sugar
¼ cup flour
½ teaspoon salt
2½ cups rhubarb, chopped into small pieces

CRUST: Preheat oven to 350 degrees. Blend crust ingredients and press into 12 × 9-inch or 13 × 9-inch pan. Bake 15 minutes.

FILLING: Mix filling ingredients and pour into baked crust. Bake 35 minutes. Makes 12 servings.

NOTE: This is a lot like pie. To make dessert more like a bar, increase the flour in filling by 1 tablespoon.

Caramel Dipping Sauce

For summer treats

1 (14-ounce) package caramels (48)
2 tablespoons creamy peanut butter
2 tablespoons water

Microwave ingredients in microwave-safe bowl on high 2½ to 3½ minutes or until smooth, stirring every minute. Serve as a dip with fresh fruit or as a sauce over ice cream or cake. Makes 1½ cups.

Creme Crepes

See Back-to-Back Brunches for Twelve, p. 257.

Dessert Kabobs

Angel food cake (or marshmallows)
Egg whites
Coconut
Banana chunks
Butter
Ground nuts
Orange wedges
Grapes

Dip chunks of cake in lightly beaten egg whites and roll in coconut. Dip banana chunks in butter and roll in ground nuts. Alternate on thin skewers with orange wedges and grapes. Grill lightly, turning once.

You might want to run this under the broiler instead of grilling, because angel food cake is fragile. For outdoor grilling, you can use marshmallows, dipped in butter and coconut, instead of cake.

Grandma's Caramel Apples

Always a hit!

1 cup butter
2 cups firmly packed light brown sugar
1 cup light corn syrup
1 (14-ounce) can sweetened condensed milk
1 teaspoon vanilla extract
8 to 10 medium apples

Melt butter in 3-quart heavy saucepan. Stir in sugar, corn syrup, and condensed milk; mix well. Bring to boiling over medium heat, stirring frequently. Cook to firm-ball stage (245 degrees), about 15 to 20 minutes, stirring frequently.

Remove from heat; stir in vanilla. Put a wooden stick in each apple at core. Dip apple into caramel mixture to cover. Place on waxed paper to allow caramel to set. Store in cool, dry place at room temperature.

(Refrigeration makes caramel too hard to eat.) Use within 2 or 3 days. Makes 8 to 10 apples.

Luscious Lemon Treat

CRUST
½ cup butter or margarine
1 cup flour
½ cup plus 1 tablespoon almonds or pecans, finely ground, divided

SECOND LAYER
1 cup powdered sugar
1 cup frozen whipped topping
1 (8-ounce) package cream cheese

THIRD LAYER
2 (3-ounce) packages lemon instant pudding mix
3 cups milk

TOPPING
1 cup frozen whipped topping
1 cup sour cream or plain yogurt

CRUST: Preheat oven to 400 degrees. Mix butter, flour, and ½ cup nuts together and press into 13 × 9-inch baking pan. Bake 15 minutes but be careful not to overbrown. Remove from oven and cool.

SECOND LAYER: Thoroughly beat together powdered sugar, whipped topping, and cream cheese. Spread over cooled crust.

THIRD LAYER: Mix together pudding mix and milk and spread over cream cheese layer.

TOPPING: Mix together topping ingredients and spread over top. Sprinkle with reserved 1 tablespoon ground nuts. Refrigerate. Makes 12 servings.

Molded French Creme

From Nancy Catena of San Francisco
So simple, so elegant, and so delicious

1 (¼-ounce) envelope unflavored gelatin
¼ cup water
1 cup sour cream
1 cup whipping cream
¾ cup sugar
1 (8-ounce) package cream cheese
½ teaspoon vanilla extract
Raspberry Sauce (see following recipe)

Brush mini-molds or large mold with vegetable oil. Sprinkle gelatin over water in cup and let soften. Place cup in saucepan of very hot water so gelatin will dissolve and liquify. Meanwhile, combine sour cream and whipping cream in saucepan. Beat in sugar; place over very low heat to warm. Whisk until all sugar is dissolved. Stir gelatin mixture into cream mixture. Remove from heat. Beat cream cheese in medium bowl until soft. Stir into warm cream mixture. Add vanilla and blend thoroughly. Pour into prepared mold. Chill. Large mold should chill 4 hours before serving; mini-molds should chill at least 90 minutes. Makes 8 servings.

TO MAKE IN FOOD PROCESSOR: Cut cream cheese in chunks and process until smooth. Add sour cream and process thoroughly. Heat whipping cream and sugar together until sugar dissolves; add softened gelatin and vanilla to cream-sugar mixture and pour into cream cheese–sour cream mixture in steady stream with motor on medium. Proceed as above.

NOTE: Sour cream can be cut to ½ cup with the addition of ½ cup plain yogurt, but you need slightly more gelatin to make molded creme set up. Neufchâtel cheese can be substituted for cream cheese.

Raspberry Sauce

2 (10-ounce) packages frozen raspberries or clean and rinse 3 pints fresh raspberries
½ tablespoon cornstarch
2 tablespoons orange liqueur or brandy

Push berries through sieve or puree in food processor. Strain to remove seeds. Combine cornstarch with orange liqueur to make paste; stir into raspberry mixture. Heat gently until sauce thickens. Cool and serve as a base or over Molded French Creme.

Don't talk prepared microwave meals to those Iowans who tote load after load of baked cakes, pies, quick breads, rolls, and cookies to the Iowa State Fair each year. In 1994 there were more than six thousand entries, up more than five hundred from the previous year. The "fair bug" must be genetic in some families. Lists of winners show two- and three-generation ties. Entrants come from miles away with cars, vans, station wagons, and trucks filled with yummy concoctions. They carry home ribbons, prizes, and cash—and lots of satisfaction. Perennial winner Robin Tarbell-Thomas of Centerville is a product of her mother's and grandmother's kitchens. And Joy McFarland of Ellston and her mother, Barb Kiburz of Tingley, win lots of contests. Joy's daughter, Landi, is starting to make her mark, too, in student divisions. And Joy's husband, David, has become a state fair ice cream winner.

Glazed Cardamom Pears

See Elegant Dinner for Eight, p. 246.

Pink Grapefruit Sorbet

See Elegant Dinner for Eight, p. 244.

Strawberries 'n' Lace

See Back-to-Back Brunches for Twelve, p. 256.

Tipsy Fruit

See Back-to-Back Brunches for Twelve, p. 259.

Strawberry-Date Sandwiches

See Tea Party for Twelve, p. 250.

Tempting Tiramisu

7 ladyfinger cookies
2 tablespoons coffee-flavored liqueur
2 tablespoons orange-flavored liqueur
2 tablespoons espresso coffee powder
2 teaspoons boiling water
2 cups ricotta cheese
2 tablespoons sugar
2 teaspoons vanilla extract
Unsweetened cocoa powder, for garnish

Separate ladyfinger halves. Combine liqueurs in small bowl. Drizzle over cut side of ladyfingers. Cut ladyfingers in half crosswise. Line bottom of 4 (6-ounce) custard cups or ramekins with parchment or waxed paper. Arrange ladyfinger halves upright around each custard cup.

Dissolve coffee powder in boiling water to make smooth paste. Stir into cheese. Stir in sugar and vanilla. Spoon mixture into prepared custard cups. Cover. Chill until firm. Unmold onto serving plates. Dust with cocoa powder. Makes 4 servings.

Chocolate-Mint Sweeties

See Tea Party for Twelve, p. 252.

Microwave Fudge

3 cups semisweet chocolate chips
1 (14-ounce) can sweetened condensed milk
¼ cup butter or margarine
1 cup chopped pecans (optional)

Lightly butter 8-inch square baking dish and set aside. Combine chocolate chips, condensed milk, and butter in 2-quart microwave-safe bowl. Microwave on high 3 to 6 minutes or until chocolate melts, stirring every 2 minutes. Fold in chopped nuts. Let cool slightly; pour into prepared baking dish, spreading evenly with spatula. Let stand until lukewarm, then chill until firm and cut into squares. Makes about 60 1-inch squares.

Party Planner

In this chapter, we have grouped interesting foods that are appropriate for various occasions. We have gathered the recipes for each occasion in one place to make it simple to follow the menus from start to finish. In addition, we've done a couple of sample time lines that make it easy—or at least easier—to put together a big "do." And, yes, we actually experimented to find the most hassle-free approach to our Champagne Brunch and our Elegant Dinner for Eight. But you can apply the principle to any entertainment. It's easily worth the couple of hours of planning time a week or two ahead to save frazzled nerves the day of the event.

Champagne Brunch for Twenty-Four

This is an uptown but easy—and not too costly—way to entertain a crowd. Stick with inexpensive but good champagne, and you won't have the bother of mixing drinks. You can cut your work considerably if you serve a good, regularly cured ham and don't bother with the Smithfield Ham.

Menu

Champagne
Vegetable Wreath and Dip
Pâté on Apple Slices
Stuffed Peapods
Smithfield Ham with Mustard
Rolls with Whipped Butter
Spinach Squares
Rice Ring
Avocado Slices with Thousand Island Dressing
Double Chocolate Cheesecake
Cheeses
Fruit Melange
Coffee

One week before

Polish silver.

Make chocolate leaves (for dessert garnish) and freeze.

Prepare Spinach Squares, Rice Ring, Rolls, and Double Chocolate Cheesecake and freeze.

Three days before

Shop for groceries.

Buy champagne.

Begin preparing Smithfield Ham.

Two days before

Cook chicken livers and make Pâté.

Do last-minute shopping—flowers, fresh vegetables.

Clean vegetables.

Make Thousand Island Dressing.

One day before

Pick up rented items: 24 china dinner plates, mugs, and dessert plates; one 12-inch brass pedestal cake stand; one 18-inch brass serving tray.

Finish cooking ham; bone and tie meat, if desired.

Make ham glaze.

Make Fruit Melange dip.

Make Vegetable Dip.

Prepare Vegetable Wreath; cover with plastic wrap and refrigerate.

Make Stuffed Peapods.

Make Fruit Melange; cover and refrigerate.

Arrange table linens, flowers, candles, china, silver, toothpicks, salt, and pepper on buffet table.

Chill champagne.

Day of party

Remove Double Chocolate Cheesecake, Spinach Squares, Rice Ring, and Rolls from freezer early in day.

Take ham from refrigerator and brush with glaze.

Put whipped butter and mustard on table.

Make coffee.

Whip cream and pipe onto Double Chocolate Cheesecake and decorate with chocolate leaves.

Heat ham, Spinach Squares, Rice Ring, and rolls in 350-degree oven.

Slice apples and spread with pâté.

Slice avocados and drizzle with lemon juice and Thousand Island Dressing.

Turn off oven.

Unmold Rice Ring on plate, decorate with pimiento and black olives, and return to warm oven.

Arrange Spinach Squares on platter.

Slice ham and put on platter.

Wait for first guests to arrive.

Pâté on Apple Slices

1 pound chicken livers
1 small onion, finely chopped
6 tablespoons butter, divided
¼ cup cognac
⅓ cup whipping cream
½ teaspoon salt
⅛ teaspoon ground allspice
¼ teaspoon freshly ground black pepper
⅛ teaspoon ground thyme
Unsalted butter
4 to 5 Granny Smith apples

Sauté livers with onion in 2 tablespoons butter until livers are firm but still slightly pink inside. Put livers and onion in blender or food processor. Add cognac to skillet juices and reduce to a few tablespoons, scraping up any bits of liver and onion. Add liquid and bits to livers along with cream and seasonings to blender. Process until mixture is smooth. Melt remaining 4 tablespoons of butter and add to pâté. Process until pâté is very smooth and well blended. Pack into small crocks or ramekins and cover with layer of melted unsalted butter. Chill at least 24 hours before serving. Remove from refrigerator about 45 minutes before serving. Spread on thin slices of Granny Smith apples.

NOTE: Use Granny Smith apples because they don't discolor as quickly as many other apples when exposed to air.

Vegetable Wreath and Dip

Clean and cut or break into attractive segments: cauliflower, broccoli, and celery (with strings removed); cut green bell pepper into rings; make radish roses; clean green onions. Arrange attractively on plate around bowl of dip.

Vegetable Dip

1 pint sour cream
1½ tablespoons white horseradish
1 tablespoon paprika
1 tablespoon minced shallots
1 teaspoon leaf tarragon
1 clove garlic, crushed
Salt to taste

Mix and chill thoroughly.

Stuffed Peapods

Fresh or frozen Chinese peapods
2 (8-ounce) packages light cream cheese, softened
Garlic or onion powder to taste

Blanch peapods; slit open one side with sharp knife. Mix cream cheese with garlic or onion powder. Put mixture in pastry tube and pipe into peapods. Chill.

Smithfield Ham

Smithfield-style hams are cured the old-fashioned way. This makes them more flavorful than the ordinary supermarket ham, but it also calls for extra preparation to eliminate excessive saltiness.

Soak ham in cold water 30 hours. Scrub ham and discard water. In fresh water, simmer ham 5 hours. Discard this water. Remove excessive fat from ham and, if desired, bone, slice and tie meat.

Meat may be glazed and baked just before serving, following usual method of heating cooked ham.

Remember, all this simmering and soaking will shrink your Smithfield ham, so be sure to buy one at least half-again as big as you would if buying a regular ham. If you don't want to take all the time and trouble for old-fashioned ham, use any good quality ham.

It has become a standing joke to many Iowans. Why has ham become the "funeral meat" in many towns? That's easy. You can put it in sandwiches, casseroles, or main dishes and can serve it hot or cold. If you get too much, you can freeze it for a later time.

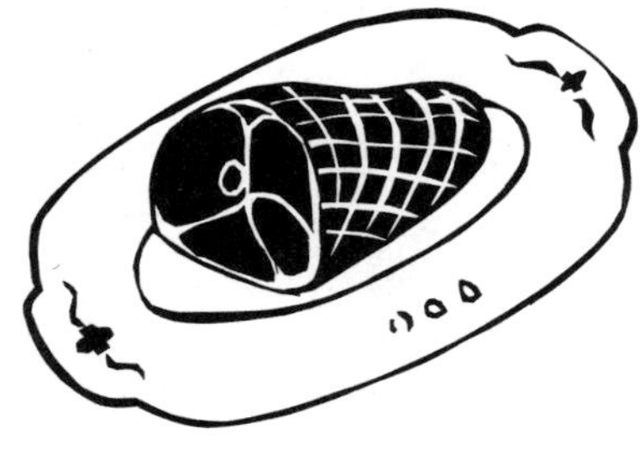

Ham Glaze

2 teaspoons dry mustard
2 tablespoons brown sugar
2 teaspoons cider vinegar

Mix and spread over ham.

Spinach Squares

4 tablespoons butter
3 eggs
1 cup flour
1 cup milk
1 teaspoon salt
1 teaspoon baking powder
1 pound Monterey Jack or Muenster cheese, grated
4 cups chopped fresh spinach or 2 (10-ounce) packages frozen chopped spinach, thawed and well drained

Preheat oven to 350 degrees. In 13 × 9 × 2-inch baking dish or—for large parties—a 15 × 10 × ¾-inch cookie sheet, melt butter in oven. In large mixing bowl, beat eggs; add flour, milk, salt, and baking powder. Mix well. Stir in cheese and spinach. Spread in pan and bake 35 minutes. Cool 30 to 40 minutes, then cut into squares. Refrigerate or freeze. To serve, bring to room temperature, preheat oven to 350 degrees, and reheat about 10 minutes.

Rice Ring

3 cups rice
6 cups chicken broth
1 teaspoon salt
1 (6-ounce) package slivered almonds
Pimientos and black olives, for garnish

Preheat oven to 350 degrees. Put rice and chicken broth in large pot with tight-fitting lid. Bring broth to boil, reduce heat, and cook on low 14 minutes or until liquid is absorbed. Let sit, tightly covered, 10 minutes or until all water has been absorbed. Meanwhile, spread slivered almonds on cookie sheet and toast in oven until lightly brown, about 8 minutes. When rice is done, mix in almonds.

Put mixture in buttered, oven-proof ring mold and refrigerate or freeze. When ready to serve, bring to room temperature, set in pan of boiling water, and bake in preheated 350-degree oven about 45 minutes. Turn out on plate and decorate with pimientos and black olives.

Avocado Slices with Thousand Island Dressing

Ripe avocados
Lemon juice
Thousand Island Dressing (see following recipe)

Slice avocados and squeeze lemon juice over slices to prevent discoloration. Drizzle Thousand Island Dressing over top.

Thousand Island Dressing

From Jennifer Phelps of Carlisle, Iowa

1 cup mayonnaise
½ cup chili sauce
1 tablespoon lemon juice
1 hard-cooked egg, chopped
¼ cup green bell pepper, finely chopped
¼ cup pimiento-stuffed olives, finely chopped

Combine ingredients and refrigerate. Makes about 2 cups.

Double Chocolate Cheesecake

You need two of these to serve twenty-four guests. Make two batches; do not double recipe.

CRUST
1 (8½-ounce) package chocolate wafers
Pinch of salt
Pinch of cinnamon
⅓ cup unsalted butter, melted

CHEESECAKE
13 ounces semisweet chocolate
1½ pounds cream cheese, at room temperature
1 cup sugar
3 eggs
2 tablespoons unsalted butter, melted
1 cup whipping cream
1 teaspoon vanilla extract

Preheat oven to 325 degrees. Crush wafers; mix in salt and cinnamon. Add butter and toss. Spoon into 9-inch springform pan and press over bottom and slightly up sides. Chill 10 minutes.

Melt chocolate over very hot water in double boiler. Cream together cheese and sugar; beat until sugar is dissolved. Add eggs but don't overmix. Add melted chocolate, butter, cream, and vanilla. Mix until smooth and lump-free. Pour into wafer crust and bake 45 minutes to 1 hour or until firm. Turn off heat and leave in oven another 30 minutes.

NOTE: Both crust and cheesecake can be made in food processor.

Chocolate Leaves

Rose leaves, from your florist
Semisweet chocolate chips, melted

Melt chocolate in double boiler set over low heat. Hold leaf at stem end and dip into chocolate. Swirl until thoroughly coated. Put on cookie sheet to harden. Dip as many as you want to decorate top of cheesecake. Leave on cookie sheet and set on freezer shelf until well hardened. Store carefully in airtight plastic container.

Fruit Melange

Fresh pineapple
Kiwi fruit
Pomegranate seeds
Mandarin oranges

Clean and cut fresh pineapple into spears. Pare and cut kiwi fruit into rounds. Open pomegranate and pop out seeds. Drain 2 cans of mandarin oranges. Put mixed fruit in clear glass bowl. Serve with long toothpicks and fruit dip.

DIP: Mix sour cream, honey, orange juice, and orange rind to taste.

Elegant Dinner for Eight

When you decide to hold a rather formal dinner, recruit a spouse or close friend to help. Or maybe a trusted baby-sitter or your own teenager would be willing to help for two or three hours and a reasonable fee. Having a helper in the kitchen makes it a lot easier to enjoy your own party.

Menu

Artichoke Rumakis
Consommé Ridgeway
Dry Sherry
Hearts of Palm Salad
Pink Grapefruit Sorbet
Veal Roll
Chablis
Composed Vegetables
Glazed Cardamom Pears
Coffee

Three days before

Check staples; make shopping list.
Order flowers for table.
Buy meats, groceries, and wine.
Wash china and crystal for table; polish silver.

Two days before

Make chicken stock for consommé and refrigerate.
Make candied orange peel.
Make Pink Grapefruit Sorbet; cover; store in freezer.

One day before

Make Consommé Ridgeway and refrigerate.
Cook Veal Roll; make sauce; refrigerate separately.
Bake pears.

Clean salad greens and refrigerate.
Prepare salad dressing and refrigerate.
Clean ingredients for Composed Vegetables and refrigerate.
Prepare orange peel.
Make Artichoke Rumakis and refrigerate.

Morning of dinner

Chill sherry in refrigerator.
Pick up flowers for the table.
Set table.

Afternoon of dinner

Slice Veal Roll; arrange slices on heat-proof platter, cover, and refrigerate.
Cook and mash potatoes for Composed Vegetables.
Steam vegetables for Composed Vegetables and put in individual ramekins.
Make sauce for Glazed Cardamom Pears.
Arrange salads on individual plates, leaving off dressing and walnuts; cover with plastic wrap; refrigerate.
Toast walnuts; do not refrigerate.

6 P.M.

Make coffee.
Put chablis in refrigerator to chill.
Remove slices of Veal Roll from refrigerator.
Take Artichoke Rumakis from refrigerator.

6:45 P.M.

Put Artichoke Rumakis in oven. Broil, turning once, until bacon is cooked.
Turn oven to 350 degrees.

7 P.M.

Greet guests; serve appetizers and drinks.

7:15 P.M.

Put Consommé Ridgeway on to simmer.

Put toasted walnuts, uncovered, in preheated 350-degree oven to warm up; check in 5 minutes to see if warm.

Pour ice water and sherry.

Pour consommé into bowls and set at individual places.

7:30 P.M.

Seat guests at table.

Remove salads from refrigerator, uncover, add dressing and warm walnuts.

Put veal sauce on stove to simmer.

7:45 P.M.

Remove consommé dishes and sherry from table.

Serve salad.

Cover platter of Veal Roll with foil, put in preheated 350-degree oven.

Take Pink Grapefruit Sorbet out of freezer.

7:55 P.M.

Put Composed Vegetables in preheated 350-degree oven.

Remove pears from refrigerator.

8 P.M.

Dish up Pink Grapefruit Sorbet.

8:05 P.M.

Remove salad plates from table.

Serve Pink Grapefruit Sorbet.

Uncork chablis.

Remove Veal Roll from oven and arrange on dinner plates.

Remove Composed Vegetables from oven, turn out on dinner plates.

Ladle veal sauce over slices of Veal Roll.

8:15 P.M.

Remove sorbet dishes from table.

Pour chablis.

Take laden dinner plates to table.

8:35 P.M.

Arrange pears on dessert plates, add sauce, and garnish with threads of candied orange peel.

8:45 P.M.

Remove dinner plates from table.

Serve pears.

Set out cream and sugar, coffee cups.

9 P.M.

Serve coffee away from the table.

Artichoke Rumakis

So easy, so good

1 (13¾-ounce) can artichoke hearts, drained
1 pound sliced bacon
Seasoned salt

Cut artichoke hearts into bite-sized pieces, dust with seasoned salt (onion is best), wrap with half-strips of bacon held in place with toothpicks, and broil until the bacon is cooked.

Consommé Ridgeway

2 cucumbers, diced
2 tablespoons fresh mint, chopped
6 cups rich chicken stock, all traces of fat removed
2 tablespoons shallots, finely chopped

1 cup tomato juice
6 drops Tabasco sauce
2 tablespoons freshly squeezed lemon juice
Salt and freshly ground black pepper to taste
8 thin slices of cucumber, for garnish

Combine cucumbers, mint, and water in saucepan. Simmer over low heat 30 minutes. Strain liquid and discard cucumber pulp and mint. Combine cucumber-mint essence with chicken stock, shallots, tomato juice, Tabasco, and lemon juice. Add salt and pepper to taste. Bring soup to boil, reduce heat, and simmer over low heat 25 minutes. Remove from heat and strain. Allow to cool. Store in refrigerator until serving time.

To serve, bring to simmer and ladle into bowls. Garnish with slice of cucumber in each bowl.

Hearts of Palm Salad

1 bunch red leaf lettuce
2 bunches Bibb or Boston lettuce
1 (14-ounce) can hearts of palm
4 ounces Roquefort cheese
1 large bunch fresh parsley, chopped

DRESSING
2 cups peanut oil
1 cup rice vinegar
¼ cup sugar
1 clove garlic, minced
Salt and freshly ground black pepper to taste

GARNISH
2 tablespoons butter
1 (6-ounce) package English walnut halves

Arrange red leaf lettuce on 8 individual salad plates. Tear Bibb or Boston lettuce into bite-sized pieces and arrange in center of red leaf lettuce. Cut hearts of palm lengthwise into thin spears and arrange in spokelike pattern on lettuce. Sprinkle chunks of cheese and parsley on salad. Cover salads with plastic wrap and store in refrigerator.

DRESSING: Combine dressing ingredients and blend well. Store dressing in refrigerator.

GARNISH: Melt butter in small skillet. Add walnuts and sauté over medium heat until browned. Do not refrigerate. To serve, warm walnuts 5 to 10 minutes in 300-degree oven. Drizzle dressing over salads. Top with warm toasted walnuts.

Pink Grapefruit Sorbet

From Jennifer Phelps of Carlisle, Iowa

2 cups sugar
1 cup water
2 cups freshly squeezed pink grapefruit juice
Juice of 2 lemons
Few drops red food coloring

Combine sugar and water in small saucepan. Bring to boil and cook 5 minutes. Remove from heat. Combine simple syrup, grapefruit juice, lemon juice, and red food coloring. Freeze mixture until firm, stirring occasionally. When thoroughly frozen, process mixture in food processor until very smooth. Return to freezer.

Veal Roll

3 eggs, well beaten
½ cup finely chopped parsley
½ cup grated Gruyère cheese
1 boned breast of veal
Salt and freshly ground black pepper to taste
2 tablespoons olive oil

2 tablespoons butter
1 medium onion, chopped
1 cup dry white wine

Combine eggs, parsley, and cheese. Make two large flat omelets. Sprinkle veal with salt and pepper. Arrange omelets on top of veal, trimming to fit. Roll veal and tie with kitchen string. Combine oil and butter in Dutch oven. Add onion and sauté until light brown. Remove onion and reserve. Add veal roll and brown on all sides. Return browned onion to pan. Add wine, cover, and simmer very gently 1½ hours.

Remove meat from pan, scraping off sauce. Pour sauce into blender and blend until smooth. Store veal roll and sauce separately in refrigerator. When meat is well chilled, cut in thin slices and arrange on serving platter.

To serve, cover platter with foil and warm meat in preheated 350-degree oven 20 minutes. Warm sauce separately on top of stove and ladle over meat.

Composed Vegetables

1½ pounds green beans of uniform size
3 large carrots
2 very small zucchini
8 fresh brussels sprouts
8 cabbage leaves
Salt and freshly ground black pepper to taste
Softened butter
¾ cup frozen green peas
4 cups mashed potatoes

Trim beans. Peel carrots and cut in julienne strips. Cut zucchini in thin slices. Steam beans 3 to 5 minutes and season with salt and pepper to taste. Repeat with carrot strips, brussels sprouts, cauliflower, and cabbage, steaming each vegetable separately 3 to 5 minutes and seasoning with salt and pepper to taste.

Generously butter 8 individual ramekins. (Be sure to use enough butter to hold vegetables in place.) Around inside bottom edge of each mold, arrange a circular border of frozen green peas. Arrange several overlapping slices of zucchini in center of circle. Stand alternate strips of carrot and green beans upright on peas and leaning against sides of molds. With fingers, press mashed potatoes firmly against sides and bottom of ramekins to form a layer to hold vegetables in place. With kitchen scissors, trim ends of carrots and beans even with top edge of ramekins. Press half a cabbage leaf into bottom of ramekin on top of mashed potatoes, trimming to fit. Add brussels sprout and cauliflower floret (1 or more of each) to fill center of each ramekin, then cover with remaining half of cabbage leaf. Top with another layer of mashed potatoes.

To serve, bake in preheated 350-degree oven 20 minutes or until vegetables are done. (You can test with thin pick.) Remove from oven and unmold on serving platter or individual dinner plates.

Glazed Cardamom Pears

From Jennifer Phelps of Carlisle, Iowa

1 whole pear per person (up to 8 pears)
⅔ cup water
⅓ cup brown sugar
⅓ cup honey
1 teaspoon ground cardamom
3 tablespoons butter

SAUCE
1 cup sour cream
⅓ cup honey
Grated peel of 1 orange (about 1 tablespoon)
1 cup whipping cream
Thin slivers of plain or candied orange peel, for garnish (see following recipe)

Preheat oven to 450 degrees. Peel, halve, and core pears. Place close together in shallow baking pan, cut-side up. Pour water in pan. Mix brown sugar, honey, and cardamom together and spoon into each pear cavity. Dot pear halves with butter. Bake 30 minutes or until pears are tender when pierced with fork. Baste fruit occasionally during baking; add water to pan if necessary. At this point pears can be refrigerated 1 day ahead of serving time.

SAUCE: Blend sour cream, honey, and orange peel. Whip cream and fold into sour cream mixture. Chill at least 1 hour. When ready to serve, top each pear half with dollop of sauce. Garnish with orange peel slivers.

Candied Orange Peel

With thanks to Irma S. Rombauer and Marion Rombauer Becker in Joy of Cooking

2 cups orange peel, white part removed as much as possible
1 tablespoon salt
Sugar

Cut peel in very thin strips. Make saline solution of 1 tablespoon salt to 4 cups water. Soak peel 24 hours in just enough salt water to cover. Drain peel. Rinse and soak in fresh water an additional 20 minutes. Drain. Cover with fresh water and boil 20 minutes. Drain again. Measure sugar to equal amount of peel. Cook sugar and peel—adding small amount of water only if necessary—until peel has absorbed sugar, stirring or shaking pan constantly to prevent burning. Spread peel out and allow to dry thoroughly. Store in air-tight container.

Tea Party for Twelve

Everything old is new again, and that certainly goes for tea parties. They're a pleasant way to entertain on a weekend afternoon and leave time for a concert or play afterward. And because the refreshments are fairly light, there will be plenty of room for supper later.

Menu

Tea
Old-Fashioned Biscuits
Currant Jelly
Ginger Preserves
Grapefruit Marmalade
Honey
Butter Curls
Cucumber Sandwiches
Radish Sandwiches
Salmon Spread Sandwiches
Strawberry-Date Sandwiches
Lemon Tart Miniatures
Pecan Tart Miniatures
Irish Whiskey Cake
Chocolate Mint Sweeties

Brewing the Tea

Preheat teapot by pouring in boiling water. While pot warms, fill teakettle with fresh, cold water and bring to rolling boil. Always start with fresh water; it contains more oxygen, which enhances tea flavor.

Empty teapot, add tea leaves, and take teapot to the kettle. Remove kettle from heat the moment water begins to boil; otherwise, flavor-enhancing oxygen is lost.

Pour boiling water over tea, cover teapot, and brew 3 to 5 minutes. Tea must have time to infuse fully, but steeping longer than 5 minutes can produce bitter taste. If you prefer weak tea, steep tea at least 3 minutes, then dilute to taste with boiling water. When brewing single cup of tea, cover teacup during steeping to promote better flavor extraction.

Old-Fashioned Biscuits

2 cups flour
½ teaspoon baking powder

½ teaspoon baking soda
½ teaspoon salt
¼ cup butter, cut into small chunks
¾ cup buttermilk

Preheat oven to 425 degrees. Into large bowl, sift flour, baking powder, baking soda, and salt. Blend thoroughly with fork. Cut in butter with pastry blender or case knife until butter bits are size of peas. Gradually pour in buttermilk, tossing mixture constantly with pastry blender. When dough starts to hold together, gather it into ball with your floured fingers. Turn out onto lightly floured board and knead 20 to 25 strokes. Press dough into flat circle. Roll to ½-inch thickness, dusting surface with flour if dough gets too sticky. Cut into circles with biscuit cutter dipped into flour before each cut. Transfer rounds to ungreased cookie sheet and bake 12 to 15 minutes or until nicely browned. Makes 16 2-inch-diameter biscuits.

Cucumber Sandwiches

24 slices dense white bread
2 (3½-ounce) packages pepper or herb-flavored Rondele cheese, softened
2 thinly sliced cucumbers
Caviar, cilantro sprigs, pimientos, dill, for garnish

Trim crusts from bread; cut slices into decorative shapes with cookie cutter. Spread with cheese. Arrange cucumber slices on cheese and garnish as desired. Makes 24 sandwiches.

Radish Sandwiches

24 slices dense white bread
½ cup softened butter
1 bunch small radishes, thinly sliced
Parsley

Trim crusts from bread and cut slices with 3-inch round cookie cutter. Spread with butter. Arrange radish slices on butter and garnish with parsley sprigs. Makes 24 sandwiches.

Salmon Spread Sandwiches

2 cups drained, flaked salmon
2 tablespoons minced chives
¼ cup finely chopped black olives
¼ teaspoon garlic powder
½ cup French dressing
12 slices dense white bread
Red or black caviar, capers, pimientos, and/or sliced green olives, for garnish

Blend salmon, chives, olives, garlic powder, and French dressing. Trim crusts from bread slices to square off. Cut slices in half diagonally to form triangle shapes. Spread with salmon mixture. Garnish as desired. Makes 24 open-faced sandwiches.

Strawberry-Date Sandwiches

From Jennifer Phelps of Carlisle, Iowa

⅔ cup boiling water
1 (7¼-ounce) package chopped, pitted dates
¼ cup butter
⅔ cup sugar
¼ teaspoon salt
1¾ cups sifted flour
½ teaspoon baking soda

TOPPING
2 (8-ounce) packages cream cheese, softened
1 pint firm, ripe strawberries, cut into thick slices

Preheat oven to 350 degrees. Pour boiling water over dates. Add butter, sugar, and salt and blend well. Combine flour with baking soda and add to date mixture a little at a time. Beat until well blended. Pour batter into 2 small greased loaf pans. Bake 1 hour or until firm when tested in center. Remove from pans and cool on wire rack. Cut each loaf into thin slices. Spread bread with cream cheese and top with strawberry slices. Makes 56 small, open-faced sandwiches.

Lemon Tart Miniatures

3 egg yolks
¼ cup cool water
½ cup cornstarch
1½ cups sifted sugar
⅛ teaspoon salt
1⅔ cups boiling water
⅓ cup lemon juice
Peel of 1 lemon, grated
1 tablespoon unsalted butter
36 baked (1-inch) tart shells (see recipe, p. 252)

Combine egg yolks with cool water in 2-quart saucepan. Add cornstarch, sugar, salt, and boiling water. Stir until smooth. Cook over medium heat, stirring continuously, until custard is thickened. Add lemon juice a little at a time. Blend well and simmer 5 minutes. Remove from heat and add butter. Stir until blended. Spoon into tart shells. Makes 36 tarts.

Pecan Tart Miniatures

From Jennifer Phelps of Carlisle, Iowa

2 tablespoons unsalted butter
½ cup sugar
1 cup dark Karo syrup

3 beaten eggs
1 teaspoon rum flavoring
3 cups pecan halves
36 unbaked (1-inch) tart shells (see following recipe)

Preheat oven to 400 degrees. Cream together butter and sugar. Add Karo syrup, eggs, and rum flavoring and blend well. Divide pecans evenly among tart shells. Pour filling over pecans, taking care not to fill tarts too full. Bake tarts 5 minutes. Reduce heat to 350 degrees and bake an additional 30 to 35 minutes or until filling is firm. Watch closely toward end of baking time to prevent burning. Makes 36 tarts.

Tart Shell

½ cup butter or margarine
1 (3-ounce) package cream cheese
1 cup flour

Cream butter and cream cheese. Add flour and mix thoroughly. Chill at least 30 minutes. Press evenly into miniature cups. Don't leave thick spots. Trim edges. (Dough in bulk or pressed into muffin cups freezes well.) Makes 24 tart shells.

Chocolate-Mint Sweeties

From Jennifer Phelps of Carlisle, Iowa

BOTTOM LAYER
2 ounces unsweetened chocolate
½ cup unsalted butter
2 eggs
1 cup sugar
½ cup flour

MIDDLE LAYER
3 tablespoons unsalted butter
1½ cups powdered sugar
2 tablespoons whipping cream
¾ teaspoon peppermint flavoring
1 or 2 drops green food coloring

TOP LAYER
2 ounces semisweet chocolate
2 tablespoons unsalted butter
1 teaspoon vanilla extract

BOTTOM LAYER: Preheat oven to 350 degrees. Melt chocolate and butter together over hot water. Beat eggs and sugar together until thick. Add chocolate mixture. Stir in flour and blend well. Pour batter into greased 9-inch square pan. Bake 25 minutes. Cool.

MIDDLE LAYER: Soften butter. Add powdered sugar, cream, and flavoring and blend until smooth. Blend in green food coloring. Spread filling evenly over cooled cake layer. Cover and chill until firm, about 1 hour.

TOP LAYER: Melt together chocolate and butter over hot water. Stir in vanilla. Drizzle glaze over mint cream filling, taking care not to completely cover mint layer with chocolate. Cover and chill again until firm. Cut into bite-sized squares and place in paper candy cups. Makes 81 1-inch cakes.

Irish Whiskey Cake

From Jennifer Phelps of Carlisle, Iowa

CAKE
1 cup sliced almonds
1 (18½-ounce) package yellow cake mix
1 (3¾-ounce) package vanilla instant pudding mix
4 eggs
½ cup cold water

½ cup salad oil
½ cup Irish whiskey

GLAZE
¼ cup butter
¼ cup water
1 cup sugar
½ cup Irish whiskey

CAKE: Preheat oven to 325 degrees. Grease and flour 12-cup Bundt pan. Spread almonds in bottom of pan. Combine remaining cake ingredients. Beat until well blended. Pour batter over nuts. Bake cake 1 hour or until cake tester comes out clean. Remove from pan and invert onto serving plate.

GLAZE: Melt butter in small saucepan. Add water and sugar and boil 5 minutes. Remove from heat and add whiskey. Prick top and sides of cake. Drizzle glaze over cake until all glaze is absorbed. Makes 24 servings.

Talk that talk. Jean Tallman, who was food editor of *The Des Moines Tribune,* the late sister paper to the *Register,* for many years and who now lives in Florida, tells of her encounter with Ken MacDonald, former publisher, the first time she used the word "brunch," a leisurely blend of breakfast and lunch. "What do you mean, 'brunch'? What does that mean and where did you come up with it? What is the meaning of that word?"

Back-to-Back Brunches for Twelve

For the energetic only. This was conceived by one of the authors who had limited space and time for entertaining but owed hospitality to a wildly diverse group of friends. She did one frenzied spate of house-cleaning, made one massive sweep through the grocery stores, used several menu items for both brunches (and made them all at once)—and survived. Both brunches were a success, but it must be admitted that by 4 P.M. Sunday, after the last guest had gone, the hostess headed straight for bed. It might be quite a bit easier if you had the help of a spouse, child, or friend.

Saturday menu

Mimosa Cocktails
Strawberries 'n' Lace
Eggs Florentine
Ham Slices
Stuffin' Muffins
Creme Crepes
Coffee

Sunday menu

Mimosa Cocktails
Tipsy Fruit
Zucchini Frittata
Rolled Ham Slices
Stuffin' Muffin
Creme Crepes
Coffee

Mimosa Cocktails

Champagne
Orange juice, preferably freshly squeezed
Fresh strawberries for garnish (optional)

In chilled wine goblet, mix about 6 ounces chilled champagne with 3 ounces chilled orange juice. Garnish with strawberry, if desired.

Strawberries 'n' Lace

1 cup sifted powdered sugar
1 teaspoon uncooked egg white
¼ teaspoon fresh lemon juice
A few drops of cognac or more lemon juice (as needed)
24 large strawberries with stems left on, washed and lain on rack

Combine sugar, egg white, and lemon juice in small, high-sided mixing bowl and beat 1 minute or more with electric mixer or wire whip until mixture forms stiff peaks. Thin, if need be, with drop or two of cognac or more lemon juice. (Icing should be thick enough to cling to strawberries.)

Holding berry by its stem end, dip in frosting to cover most of sides; replace on rack. Make 1 hour or so in advance. May be served alone or as garnish for desserts or ice cream.

Stuffin' Muffins

2 cups whole wheat flour
2 teaspoons baking powder
½ teaspoon salt
¼ to ½ cup honey
¼ cup vegetable oil
1 beaten egg or egg white
1½ cups milk

Preheat oven to 400 degrees. Combine dry ingredients in large bowl. In smaller bowl, combine wet ingredients, add fruits or fillings, and mix. Add to dry ingredients and mix until wet. Pour into lightly greased or paper-lined muffin cups. Do not fill more than ⅔ full. Bake 20 minutes or until brown. Makes 24 muffins.

VARIATIONS

Fruit Muffins: Add 1 to 2 cups blueberries or cranberries (frozen, canned, or fresh).

Sour Cream Muffins: Add 8 ounces sour cream in addition to rest of ingredients.

Buttermilk Muffins: Substitute 1½ cups buttermilk for regular milk; use only 1 teaspoon baking powder and add 1 teaspoon baking soda.

Peanut Butter Muffins: Add 16-ounce jar of peanut butter.

NOTE: The basic recipe makes delicious whole wheat muffins, but you can experiment with other interesting ingredients to come up with your own creations.

Creme Crepes

2 eggs
½ cup flour
¼ cup sugar
2 tablespoons unsweetened cocoa powder
1 cup milk
1 tablespoon melted butter
1 teaspoon vanilla extract

FILLING
2 cups (12 ounces) semisweet chocolate chips
1½ teaspoons vanilla extract
Pinch of salt
1½ cups whipping cream, heated to boiling
6 egg yolks
(2 egg whites)
Whipped cream and toasted almonds, for garnish

CREPES: In blender (not food processor), combine crepe ingredients at low speed about 30 seconds or until mixed (don't overblend). If using electric mixer, combine eggs and flour, add sugar and cocoa powder, and gradually pour in milk, beating continuously and scraping sides of bowl. Add butter and vanilla and beat until well mixed. Allow batter to stand, covered, at least 1 hour before making crepes.

Place 8-inch crepe pan or skillet over high heat and brush lightly with butter. When butter is sizzling but not brown, pour about ¼ cup batter into pan. Quickly lift pan off heat and swirl to coat bottom and sides, pouring excess batter back into bowl. Return to heat and cook about 1 minute or until bottom darkens slightly and looks dry. (Watch carefully to prevent burning.) Turn crepe onto paper towel or waxed paper. Continue until all batter is used, brushing pan with butter as needed.

When crepes are cooled, place about 1 heaping tablespoon filling on each and roll cigar-fashion. Place seam-side down on baking sheet and freeze. When firm, wrap carefully and keep in freezer until ready to thaw and serve. When frozen crepes are thawed, top with whipped cream and sliced almonds.

FILLING: Combine chocolate, vanilla, and salt in blender or food processor fitted with steel knife and mix 30 seconds. Add hot cream and continue mixing 30 seconds more or until chocolate is completely melted. Add yolks and mix about 5 seconds. Transfer to bowl and allow to cool. Spoon into crepes.

NOTE: If you plan to serve crepes without freezing them, 2 egg whites should be beaten until stiff peaks form and gently folded into chocolate filling mixture.

Zucchini Frittata

From Nancy Catena of San Francisco

4 green onions, sliced
Oil for sautéing
8 eggs
1 cup half-and-half cream
¾ teaspoon salt
1 to 2 (4½-ounce) cans chopped green chilies
1 tablespoon butter
2 cups shredded zucchini, squeezed very dry
2½ cups grated Monterey Jack cheese, divided

Cook and stir onions in oil until tender. Beat eggs with half-and-half and salt until fluffy. Stir in sautéed onions, green chilies, zucchini, and 2 cups cheese. Pour into lightly oiled 13 × 9-inch baking dish. May be made ahead and refrigerated until ready to bake. Before serving, bake in preheated 350-degree oven 25 to 30 minutes. Sprinkle remaining ½ cup of cheese on top and continue to bake until cheese melts.

Eggs Florentine

4 (10-ounce) packages frozen spinach
1 (10¾-ounce) can cream of mushroom soup
Approximately 14 eggs
2 cups grated Cheddar cheese
Butter

Preheat oven to 350 degrees. Cook spinach. Don't overcook and don't salt. Drain thoroughly and mix with enough soup to moisten. (Soup may be thinned with milk, if necessary.) Make bed of spinach mixture in bottom of lightly greased 13 × 9-inch casserole. With bottom of small juice glass, press rows of indentations into spinach. Break eggs into each depression, being careful not to break yolks. Dot top of each egg with dab of butter and sprinkle cheese thickly over top. Bake approximately 30 minutes or until egg whites are cooked.

Tipsy Fruit

Cut up a variety of fruits (fresh, frozen, and/or canned)—fresh strawberries, blueberries, pineapple, kiwi, bananas. Sprinkle liberally with kirsch brandy. Allow fruit to macerate in covered bowl in refrigerator for several hours. Serve in small dishes and pour champagne over each serving to add sparkle and fizz.

Pizza Party for Eight

This is a winner for guests of all ages or when the family feels like stirring up a little fun. Kids and adults alike will enjoy concocting their own favorite flavors of pizza pie.

Make-Your-Own Pizza

CRUSTS
1 (16-ounce) package hot roll mix
1¼ cups hot water (120 to 130 degrees)
2 tablespoons vegetable oil
Cornmeal (optional)

TOPPINGS
1 (15-ounce) can pizza sauce
2½ ounces (½ cup) pepperoni slices, cut in half
8 ounces bulk Italian sausage, cooked
8 ounces (2 cups) shredded mozzarella cheese
½ cup sliced green or black olives
½ cup sliced green onions
1 (6-ounce) jar artichoke hearts
6 ounces (2 cups) sliced fresh mushrooms
Red or green bell pepper rings
2 tablespoons chopped fresh basil or 2 teaspoons dried basil
Any other toppings you like

CRUSTS: Preheat oven to 425 degrees. In large bowl, combine flour mixture and yeast from hot roll mix; mix well. Stir in water and oil until dry particles are moistened. Turn dough out onto floured surface. With greased or floured hands, knead dough 5 minutes, until smooth. Follow directions on back of hot roll mix package for kneading.

Generously grease two cookie sheets. For crisper crust, sprinkle sheets with cornmeal. Divide dough into 8 pieces and pat into 8 (6-inch) circles on cookie sheets; turn up dough around edges of individual pizza circles. Generously prick bottom of each circle with fork. Cover dough with plastic wrap or towel. Let rise 15 minutes.

Uncover dough. Bake 6 to 10 minutes or until slightly browned. Remove from cookie sheets and cool on racks. Wrap in airtight package and refrigerate up to 2 weeks or freeze up to 2 months.

TOPPINGS: Top each crust with pizza sauce and choice of toppings. Bake in preheated 425-degree oven 6 to 10 minutes or until crust is golden brown and cheese is melted.

Holiday Dinner

Some things are so steeped in tradition, you just can't ignore them. It wouldn't seem like Thanksgiving, for instance, without turkey, cranberries, and pumpkin. Here we've tried a few variations on the usual theme by adding a spicy glaze on the turkey, zipping up the cranberries with some pineapple, and serving the pumpkin in the form of a delicious cheesecake. Even the sweet potatoes are a little different.

Menu

Hot Cranberry Punch
Roast Turkey with Spiced Currant Glaze
Cornbread Dressing
Potatoes with Chives
Sweet Potato Skillet
Cranberry-Pineapple Relish
Snap Peas with Pearl Onions
Orange-Onion Salad
Pumpkin Cheesecake

Hot Cranberry Punch

6 cups cranberry juice cocktail
⅓ cup pineapple juice
⅓ cup brown sugar
½ teaspoon cinnamon
½ teaspoon ground cloves

Put ingredients in percolator coffeepot and stir to blend. Brew as for coffee. Or simply heat in large pot on top of stove. If desired, rum may be added before serving. Makes 10 servings.

Roast Turkey

18- to 20-pound turkey, fresh or frozen
½ cup butter, divided
Garnishes (optional)

Preheat oven to 325 degrees. Remove giblets (liver, gizzard, heart, and neck, usually found in paper packets tucked into breast and neck cavities of bird) and discard or simmer until tender in water and use to flavor turkey gravy or soup later. Lightly brush bottom of roasting pan with oil. Turn wing tips under turkey. Rub turkey breast lightly with ¼ cup butter. Place turkey, breast-side up, in oven about 5 to 5½ hours before serving. Baste bird occasionally with remaining ¼ cup melted butter and then with its own juices. After 3 hours of cooking time, test turkey with meat thermometer inserted in thickest part of thigh and breast. Last 15 minutes of roasting time, brush with Spiced Currant Glaze (see following recipe). Turkey is done when meat thermometer registers 175 to 185 degrees, depending on personal preference. When turkey is done, remove from oven and let sit about 30 minutes before slicing. Garnish with small polished apples, sliced or whole oranges, or bunches of grapes, if desired.

Turkey Tips

A frozen turkey should be completely thawed in the refrigerator before you put it in the oven to roast. For a 12-pound turkey, allow 2 days; for a 24-pound turkey, allow 3 to 4 days.

TRADITIONAL ROAST TURKEY: Preheat oven to 325 degrees. Roast turkey, breast-side up, basting hourly with oil or butter and, later, pan juices. Here is timing for stuffed, chilled birds:

8 to 12 pounds: 4¾ to 5½ hours
12 to 16 pounds: 5½ to 6¼ hours
16 to 20 pounds: 6¼ to 8¾ hours
20 to 24 pounds: 8¾ to 10½ hours

Test for doneness by piercing thick part of thigh; juices should run clear. Or insert meat thermometer between thigh and body of bird; temperature should be 175 to 185 degrees, depending on personal preference. After the turkey is taken from the oven, it should sit about 30 minutes before it is carved.

QUICK ROAST TURKEY: Preheat oven to 450 degrees. Wrap bird completely in foil. Put in large roasting pan, breast-side up. Roast at constant 450-degree temperature. Times listed below are for unstuffed, chilled turkey. Add 30 to 45 minutes if turkey is stuffed.

8 to 10 pounds: 2¼ to 2½ hours
10 to 12 pounds: 2¾ to 3 hours
14 to 16 pounds: 3 to 3¼ hours
18 to 20 pounds: 3¼ to 3½ hours
22 to 24 pounds: 3½ to 3¾ hours

For an elegant Thanksgiving meal I once published a recipe for Truffled Turkey. In this case, truffles, of course, referred to the exotic and much prized fungi that grow underground and are sniffed out by trained pigs and truffle hounds. A reader, though, called with a basic question. Did it matter what flavor of truffle—as in chocolate candy truffle—was used? The thought of melting chocolate truffles with a big golden bird is more than I dared to contemplate.

Spiced Currant Glaze

¼ cup red currant jelly
1 tablespoon lemon juice
1 tablespoon butter or margarine
1½ teaspoons cornstarch
Dash of salt
¼ teaspoon ground cinnamon
1 tablespoon vinegar

In saucepan, combine jelly, lemon juice, and butter; heat and stir until jelly melts. Combine cornstarch, salt, and cinnamon; blend in vinegar. Stir into jelly mixture; cook and stir until thickened and bubbly. Brush over poultry last 15 minutes of roasting. Makes ⅓ cup.

Make-ahead Corn Bread Dressing

CORN BREAD
2 cups yellow cornmeal
2 cups flour
3 tablespoons sugar
1 teaspoon salt
4 teaspoons baking powder
½ cup vegetable oil
2 cups milk
2 eggs

DRESSING
2 green bell peppers, seeded and cut into chunks
2 medium onions, cut into eighths
4 stalks celery, cut into 2-inch lengths
2 apples, unpeeled, cored, and quartered
1 bunch parsley, including part of stems, rinsed and dried
1 to 1½ pounds crumbled sausage (as spicy as you like)
4 tablespoons vegetable oil, divided
2 teaspoons ground nutmeg

1 tablespoon ground thyme
1 tablespoon ground sage
1 teaspoon ground oregano
Salt to taste

CORN BREAD: Preheat oven to 400 degrees. In mixing bowl, combine and stir together dry ingredients. In deeper bowl, combine oil, milk, and eggs and beat until frothy. Add liquid ingredients to dry ones and blend; may be a bit lumpy.

Grease 2 8- or 9-inch square baking pans. Divide batter evenly between pans and bake until golden brown and wooden pick or metal skewer inserted in center comes out clean, 20 to 25 minutes. Remove corn bread from oven and cool. Turn out on cutting board and cut each square into slices about ½ inch thick. Lay slices flat and dice into ½-inch squares. Put corn bread pieces in mixing bowl, cover, and leave overnight.

DRESSING: In blender or food processor with metal blade, combine peppers, onions, celery, apples, and parsley. Pulse motor on and off until everything is nicely chopped but not pulverized or chop ingredients with knife. Reserve.

In 12-inch skillet, sauté sausage in 2 tablespoons oil until browned, 15 to 20 minutes. Drain and reserve sausage. Add remaining 2 tablespoons oil in same skillet over medium heat. When liquid begins to bubble, add reserved chopped vegetables and apples and toss. Cover, reduce heat to low, and cook vegetables until translucent and soft, 20 minutes or less. Remove from heat and cool.

Combine cooled vegetable mixture, sausage, and corn bread. Add dressing spices and herbs and mix, lifting and turning gently. Adjust seasonings. Put dressing in zip-top plastic bags or into buttered shallow baking pan or casserole. Close bags or cover casserole tightly and freeze or keep in refrigerator 3 to 4 days.

Two days before serving, remove dressing from freezer and place in refrigerator to thaw. About 6 hours before serving, put dressing into buttered shallow baking dish; leave on counter near stove.

After turkey has been roasting 1 hour, begin basting dressing with liquid from turkey roasting pan. You will probably add about 2 cups, so that dressing is fairly moist but not soupy.

After turkey is removed from oven, put uncovered baking dish of dressing in oven at 300 to 350 degrees and bake until top feels slightly dry to the touch and begins to brown a little, 30 to 35 minutes.

Potatoes with Chives

8 medium baking potatoes (about 2 pounds), peeled and cut into ½-inch pieces
1 cup hot milk
3 tablespoons fresh chopped chives or green onion tops
3 tablespoons melted butter
4 tablespoons grated Parmesan cheese
Salt and pepper to taste

Cook potatoes in boiling water to cover 10 minutes or until tender; drain. Return potatoes to saucepan and mash with potato masher. Stir in remaining ingredients. Makes 8 servings.

Sweet Potato Skillet

4 tablespoons butter, divided
2 pounds sweet potatoes, peeled and cut into ⅛-inch slices
Freshly grated or ground nutmeg to taste
Salt and freshly ground black pepper to taste

Coat bottom of nonstick 10-inch oven-proof skillet with 1 tablespoon melted butter. Arrange half of sweet potato slices in skillet, overlapping them in one layer. Sprinkle potatoes with nutmeg and salt and pepper and dot with 1 tablespoon butter. Top with remaining slices of sweet potatoes, overlapping as before. Sprinkle second layer of potatoes with nutmeg, salt, and pepper and dot with remaining 2 tablespoons butter. (Can be made several hours ahead and refrigerated, covered with foil.)

Preheat oven to 450 degrees. Cover sweet potatoes with foil and weigh down with heavy, oven-proof saucepan. Cook on stove top over moderate heat 5 minutes from time butter begins to sizzle. Transfer to oven and bake, still covered and weighted, in middle of oven 10 minutes. Carefully remove saucepan and foil and continue to bake sweet potatoes in upper third of oven 10 minutes or until tender. When done, invert platter over skillet, then invert potatoes onto platter. Cut sweet potatoes into wedges. Makes 8 servings.

Cranberry-Pineapple Relish

1 large orange, unpeeled
1 (12-ounce) package fresh cranberries, rinsed
1 (20-ounce) can crushed pineapple in juice, drained
¾ cup sugar

Cut orange into pieces. Remove seeds, if necessary. Chop orange and cranberries into coarse pieces in food processor or blender. Pour into bowl. Stir in pineapple and sugar. Cover with plastic wrap. Let stand at room temperature overnight to blend flavors, then store in refrigerator. Makes 4½ cups.

Snap Peas with Pearl Onions

3 (10-ounce) packages frozen sugar snap peas
1 (10-ounce) package frozen pearl onions
2 teaspoons butter
1 tablespoon minced fresh mint or 1 teaspoon dried mint flakes
¾ cup salted cashews

Prepare peas and onions according to package directions; drain well. In large skillet, melt butter and sauté vegetables to coat; stir in mint and mix well. Remove from heat, stir in cashews, and serve immediately. Makes 8 generous servings.

Orange-Onion Salad

5 medium oranges, peeled
1 medium red onion, peeled, thinly sliced, and separated into rings
Salad greens

DRESSING
4 tablespoons vegetable oil
2 tablespoons red wine vinegar
1 tablespoon orange juice
2 teaspoons sugar
¼ teaspoon ground cumin
¼ teaspoon cayenne pepper
Salt to taste

With sharp knife, remove all white membrane from oranges. Cut crosswise into ¼-inch-thick slices. On serving platter, arrange salad greens. Arrange orange slices and onion rings, alternating, atop greens. In small bowl, whisk together dressing ingredients. Drizzle over salad. Makes 8 servings.

Pumpkin Cheesecake

CRUST
1½ cups finely crushed Graham cracker crumbs
¼ cup ground almonds
2 tablespoons sugar
½ teaspoon ground ginger
½ teaspoon cinnamon
6 tablespoons unsalted butter, melted

FILLING
2 pounds cream cheese, softened
1¼ cups sugar
3 tablespoons cognac
3 tablespoons maple syrup
1 teaspoon ground ginger
1 teaspoon cinnamon
½ teaspoon ground nutmeg
4 eggs, at room temperature
¼ cup whipping cream
1 cup canned pumpkin

TOPPING
1⅓ cups sour cream or plain yogurt
3 tablespoons sugar
1 tablespoon cognac
1 tablespoon maple syrup
½ cup sliced almonds, toasted, for garnish

CRUST: Preheat oven to 250 degrees. Generously grease 10-inch springform pan. Combine crust ingredients. Press crumb mixture firmly into bottom of springform pan. Set aside.

FILLING: Beat cream cheese with mixer until smooth. Gradually add sugar, beating until light and fluffy. Add cognac, maple syrup, ginger, cinnamon, and nutmeg. Blend well. Add eggs, one at a time, beating well after each addition. Add cream and pumpkin. Mix well.

Pour filling into unbaked crust and smooth top. Bake 2 to 3 hours, until soft but firm. Shake pan slightly. Filling should not wiggle. Remove cheesecake from oven and let cool on rack 30 minutes. After 20 minutes, turn up oven to 350 degrees.

TOPPING: Combine sour cream, sugar, cognac, and maple syrup. Mix thoroughly. Spread topping on cooled cheesecake.

Return assembled cheesecake to oven for 7 minutes. Remove from oven and let cake cool on rack at least 4 hours at room temperature before removing sides of pan. Garnish outer edge of cake with toasted almond slices. Slice cake with warm knife.

You can make cheesecake up to 2 weeks before serving. Store tightly wrapped in freezer. Or make 2 days before serving and store tightly wrapped in refrigerator. Makes 10 to 12 servings.

Substitutions & Blends

Instead of 1 cup of the following ingredients, you can substitute as below.

YOGURT: 1 cup buttermilk or 1 tablespoon lemon juice stirred into 1 cup milk; let stand 5 minutes
BUTTERMILK: 1 cup plain yogurt or 1 tablespoon lemon juice stirred into 1 cup milk; let stand 5 minutes
SOUR CREAM: 3 tablespoons melted butter stirred into 1 cup buttermilk or 1 cup plain yogurt
WHOLE MILK: ½ cup evaporated milk mixed with ½ cup water or 2 teaspoons butter plus 1 cup skim milk or water
SOUR MILK: 1 cup buttermilk or 1 tablespoon lemon juice stirred into 1 cup milk; let stand 5 minutes
WHIPPING CREAM: ⅓ cup melted butter plus ¾ cup milk
RICOTTA CHEESE: 1 cup cottage cheese with liquid drained off

Mild Chili Blend

2 tablespoons chili powder
1 tablespoon ground cumin
1 tablespoon ground or leaf oregano
1 tablespoon garlic powder
1 tablespoon salt substitute
1 tablespoon saffron (optional)

Blend ingredients. Use in ground beef, chili, or yogurt dips.

Vegetable Blend

1½ tablespoons onion powder
1½ tablespoons toasted sesame seeds
1 tablespoon dried chives
1 tablespoon leaf tarragon
½ tablespoon dry mustard
½ tablespoon dried dillweed

½ tablespoon dried red bell pepper
½ tablespoon salt substitute

Blend ingredients. Use on vegetables and salads and in dips.

Meat Blend

2 tablespoons leaf rosemary
2 tablespoons ground savory
1 tablespoon leaf thyme
1 tablespoon ground marjoram

Blend ingredients. Use on meats and in stews.

Pseudo Seasoned Salt

1 tablespoon dry mustard
1 tablespoon garlic powder
2 teaspoons dried dillweed
2 teaspoons onion powder
2 teaspoons ground thyme
2 teaspoons paprika
2 teaspoons dried savory
1 teaspoon lemon peel

Blend ingredients. Use on vegetables and salads or in dips.

Cottage Cheese Blend

2 tablespoons dried chives
2 tablespoons parsley flakes
1 tablespoon garlic powder
1 tablespoon celery seeds
1 tablespoon dried chervil

Blend ingredients. Use on cottage cheese, in cottage cheese dips, and in mixtures such as egg salad.

Poultry Blend

2½ tablespoons ground thyme
2½ tablespoons ground sage
2 tablespoons ground marjoram

Blend ingredients. Use on poultry.

Garlic and Parsley Blend

6 tablespoons parsley flakes
2 teaspoons garlic powder or granules
1 teaspoon onion flakes
1 teaspoon paprika
1 teaspoon finely ground black pepper

Blend ingredients. Use on fish and breads and anywhere you'd use garlic.

Index

(*continued*)

(*continued*)

(*continued*)

(*continued*)

(*continued*)

(*continued*)

(*continued*)

(*continued*)

The Authors

Carol Marlow McGarvey is the food expert at *The Des Moines Register.* She's the person who knows what to substitute when you're out of cake flour and what a caper is. She handles the frantic calls from readers who have lost a favorite recipe—or who remember seeing a dish they're dying to try out but can't quite recall where. She has been at the *Register* for more than twenty years as an editor and feature writer. For six years she wrote a syndicated food column called "Let's Ask the Cook," and she has done free-lance writing for a variety of publications. In her opinion, M&Ms should be on the Food Guide Pyramid. She has bought lots of groceries for her husband, Tom, and three children, Matt, Andy, and Molly.

Marie DeLanoit McCartan, a die-hard chocolate fan, had the dirty job of testing many of the book's chocolate recipes. It's a job she's well prepared for—she has snacked at her desk for years as a writer for Younkers, Heritage Cablevision, and Kragie/Newell Advertising and while free-lancing for a number of central Iowa companies. A cookbook collector, she likes to experiment with recipes. When her husband, John, and sons Joe and Ted query her about how a new dish will taste, her response is always, "Would these hips lie?"

C. R. Mitchell had a number of short careers—hospital aide, telephone operator, secretary, publicity writer, encyclopedia salesperson, flight attendent, beachcomber, newspaper reporter, free-lance writer—before settling in as an editor at *The Des Moines Register.* Her leisure-time diversions have been equally eclectic, from "championship" jacks (the kind you play with a bouncy ball) and testing pogo sticks to reading and eating popcorn in bed. She has eaten her way through some of the world's finest restaurants, first dragging along her daughter and son and now her (strenuously objecting) two grandchildren.

Bur Oak Cookbooks

A Cook's Tour of Iowa
By Susan Puckett

The Des Moines Register *Cookbook*
By Carol McGarvey, Marie McCartan,
and C. R. Mitchell

Neighboring on the Air: Cooking with the KMA Radio Homemakers
By Evelyn Birkby

Prairie Cooks: Glorified Rice, Three-Day Buns, and Other Reminiscences
By Carrie Young with Felicia Young

Up a Country Lane Cookbook
By Evelyn Birkby